TRANSFORMED BY EATING

ROYAL JELLY

The Metamorphosis of the Human Soul

Dr. Michael H Yeager

ISBN: 9781094787282
Imprint: Independently published

DEDICATION

We dedicate this book to those who are truly hungry and thirsty to live in the realm of the super natural, and to those who have already tasted of the heavenly realm. We dedicate this to the bride of Christ, those who are called to go deeper, higher, and farther than they have yet experienced. It is only by the grace that comes by FAITH in CHRIST that we will be able to accomplish His will in this earth.

CONTENTS

Acknowledgments   i

1   Chapter One   1

2   Chapter Two   16

3   Chapter Three   36

4   Chapter Four   58

5   Chapter Five   78

6   Chapter Six   91

7   Chapter Seven   108

8   Chapter Eight   120

9   Chapter Nine   135

10 Chapter Ten   149

ACKNOWLEDGMENTS

*To our heavenly Father and His wonderful love.

*To our Lord, Savior and Master —Jesus Christ, who saved us and set us free because of His great love for us.

*To the Holy Spirit, who leads and guides us into the realm of miraculous living every day.

*To all of those who had a part in helping us get this book ready for the publishers.

*To my Wife Kathleen and our precious children, Michael, Daniel, Steven, Stephanie, Catherine Yu, who is our precious daughter-in-law, and Naomi, who is now with the Lord!

Introduction

The miraculous happenings, heavenly visitations, and divine deliverance's that you are about to read are all true. They have happened personally to my family and I. These experiences are recalled and shared to the best of our ability.

By no means do the following stories account for all the visitations and miracles of God that we have experienced in our lives. If we would recount every single answer to prayer, and every wonderful miracle and blessing, there would be no end to this book! Both my wife and I, including our children, have had numerous supernatural dreams, visions, healing s and experiences. In some of our heavenly encounters, God gave us specific information which has come to pass, as well as visions and dreams which have yet to be fulfilled.

What we are about to share with you in this book are simply some highlights of what we have experienced in the Lord. Some of these experiences will seem to be incredulous, however,

they are true. This is not a testimony of how spiritual we are, but how wonderful and marvelous the Father, the Son, and the Holy Ghost are! We share these experiences to the best of our recollections and understanding. Not every conversation we share in these experiences are exactly **WORD** for **WORD**. We would love to name every person that was a part of these wonderful occurrences, but privacy laws do not allow this. If you are reading this book and you saw, experienced, or were a part of these events, please do not be offended because your names were not mentioned.

At the end of this book there will be a brief teaching on how you can enter into a position where God will supernaturally begin to speak, lead and guide you in your life. It is God's will that all who follow Him would enter into this realm where all things are possible. What God has done for us, He will do for everyone. He is not a respecter of people.

GOD Said: You Better Not Lie, or You'll Die to!

One day I picked up a book by a well-known author. This book had come highly recommended by one of my favorite preachers at that time. The topic was about angelic visitations. This was something I was interested in, because of my many experiences with the supernatural. I began to read this book, and noticed immediately that there were experiences he said he had, which did not seem to line up with the Scriptures. I did not want to judge his heart, but we do have the responsibility to examine everything in light of God's **WORD**. If it does not line up with the **WORD** of God, then we must reject it, no matter who wrote it.

As I was pondering the stories in this book, the Spirit of the Lord spoke to my heart very strongly. It was as if He was standing right there next to me, speaking audibly. What He spoke to me was rather shocking! The Lord told me that the writer of this book would be dead in three months from a heart attack. I asked the Lord why He was telling me this. He said the stories in the man's book were exaggerated, and judgment was coming. **This man had opened the door for he devil to take him out!** The Lord warned me that day that if I were ever to do the same thing, judgment would come to me. I did not realize that the Lord would have me to be writing books, many them filled with my own personal experiences. Now I know why he spoke this to me, telling me that I better not exaggerate my experiences.

When the Spirit of the Lord spoke this to me, I turned and told my wife. I held the book up and said, in a very quiet whispering, trembling, wavering voice, "Honey, the man who wrote this book will be dead in three months from a heart attack." Plus, I told her why the Lord told me this. I wish I had been wrong. Exactly 3 months later, the man died from a heart attack. God can speak to us through the positive and the negative circumstances of life. We better take heed to what he is saying.

CHAPTER ONE

Local Bank Loan Officer All Upset

I would like to begin this book about **Eating Royal Honey** by telling you about an event that happened in 2015. I met a lady who was a loan officer at a local bank. As I was talking to her, I felt in my heart that I should give her two of my books. The one book is called: Living in the Realm of the Miraculous # 1. The second book is called: I need God because I'm stupid. Now, this particular loan officer was about my age. We finished with the business we were discussing, she went her way, and I went mine.

About a week later I received a phone call from her. I could tell that something was wrong. She was literally to the point of tears over the phone. Here's a born again, spirit filled woman. She said to me: Pastor Mike I've read your **two books**.

*I Need God Because I'm Stupid

*Living In the Realm of the Miraculous.

She said: to be honest with you I don't understand how you could live in this realm. How could you have so many experiences ? How, could you help so many people? How could you have so many miracles? How can this be?

I could tell that she was really dumbfounded! I said to her: It's not because I'm really super spiritual. It's not because I'm in prayer eight hours a day or that I go on a 40 day fast every couple of months.

I said to her: Do you want to know what it is? She said: yes, what is it? I said: I began to do something back in 1975 as a baby Christian. What's that she asked? I began to **Hide the WORD of God in My Heart**. I began to devour the tuths of the bible, God's **WORD**! That's what it is. I began to Renew My Mind with the **WORD**.

On top of that from 1975 up to 1984, I simply ate, drank, quoted and meditated on nothing but God's **WORD**. You can even ask my wife and she will tell you that for the first eight years of our marriage our main staple was nothing but God's **WORD**.

To be honest, it is not like as if we simply decided to not let anything else into our house, we just never thought of it. We did not have a TV, radio, newspapers, secular books, or worldly movies. Yes, we did listen to Gospel teaching and preaching by cassette, Christian books, and Christian music.

Romans 2:4 Or despisest thou the riches of his goodness and forbearance and longsuffering; not knowing that the goodness of God leadeth thee to repentance?

TV - Thanks but No Thanks

I remember back in 1983 I was preaching at a local church, and I just happened to mention this over the pulpit. That was on a Sunday, and by Monday morning there was someone knocking at my door. I opened the door and there was a sweet little old lady who had been at the meeting on Sunday.

She seemed to be so excited and happy. She said Pastor Mike I've got a gift for you. I said: you do? Yes, yes, I heard what you said on Sunday. What did I say, I asked? You said you didn't have a TV, so I went and got to one. To be honest with you I did not want to offend her. She must've thought I was complaining. But I was rejoicing in the fact that we did not have a TV in our house. Well, to make a long story short, I did not want to hurt her feelings. I went out to her car to get this brand-new TV which was still in its box. I took it out of her car, and carried it into our house.

We thanked her for her generosity, and kindness. This TV set in my front room in its box for a couple days, but it began to call out to me. Well, stupid is as stupid does. I finally opened up the box, and set the TV up. I adjusted the antenna that was built into the back of it. I do not know where she got the TV, but was an old black and white that was still in its box. Maybe it had been in storage for years. I was able to get a couple channels, and began to watch it. Immediately I felt my spiritual life draining out of me. I got so upset that I decided to put it away.

The next thing I knew This TV kept calling my name. And I would hollowed out again, watch it for a very little time, and then put it away. It got so bad that I said to myself: I need to put it somewhere that it will not be easy to get. The house I was living in had a small hole in the ceiling with a cover. It was access to their attic. So I hauled it up there one day.

Another day went by, and the TV began to call my name again. I found myself late at night crawling up into the attic, pulling it down, and setting it up. I tried to watch it for a little bit, and then I was so sickened, that I unplugged it and went to bed. The next day I made a donation of that TV to a local thrift store. People wonder why they have no spirituality in their lives, and it is because of feeding and foolishness.

God's WORD First Place in Our Home

When my children were little, all we fed it was God's **WORD**. Actually we never told them not to listen to secular music because we never gave them secular music. We would buy them good Christian programs, Bible stories, godly books in order to feed them they proper spiritual diet.

My two oldest sons Michael, and Daniel would listen to the Bible all day long. The name of the program was God: Your Story Hour. A Family-friendly radio drama from the Bible, historical heroes, and true-to-life adventures. Children's Audio Stories. Free Kid Activities. Character-Building Tales.

My two sons knew the **WORD** of God so well that the local churches would not allow them to attend their vacation Bible schools. Why you ask? It is because they would win all of the contest. For the first two or three years and our community they would come home with all the prizes.

By the fourth year we were informed that they were no longer welcomed. I know this sounds preposterous but it's true.

The reason why my children never messed with the drugs, alcohol, sex and filth that is in the world, like so many other preachers and Christian kids who are born again, Christians here's not because they are so spiritual. It is not because there dad who was a pastor (myself) was harping on them. Actually, if you ask them they would tell you that I never preached at them.

The reason why the devil was never able to completely mess them up like so many other Christian children is because we help them hide the **WORD** of God in their hearts.

I mean to this day if you were to visit my children when they were sleeping in their beds, most likely they will have the Bible playing. That's how they were raised from the time they were newborns. The **WORD** of God was continually playing in their bedrooms. Here it is over 30 years later, and there still doing it.

What Is Royal Jelly?

We will be teaching on the subject of what is **Spiritual Royal Jelly**. The natural world many times holds lessons for us when it comes to the spiritual world. Bees, honeybees are a wonderful example of what needs to take place in the believer's life. The difference between a Queen Honeybee and a worker bee is simply what they eat. Really Pastor Mike? Yes, incredibly it's simply their diet.

The worker bees are fed Royal Jelly for the first three days of their life after they hatch. The Queen Bee is feed nothing but Royal Jelly. That's all they feed her. And it Transforms a worker bee into a Queen. Suddenly this bee becomes a Queen and is producing all of the of the hive.

Amazing Facts = A healthy honeybee hive usually has around 20,000-50,000 bees during summer. Almost all of these will be female workers, along with a queen and a few hundred male drones. The queen's egg laying rate peaks around May-June up to 1,500 a day - at this time she lays more than her own body weight in eggs each day!

NATURAL FACTS ABOUT ROYAL JELLY

What is Spiritual ROYAL JELLY?

Royal jelly is a Special honey bee secretion that is used in the feeding of larvae, as well as adult queens.[1] It is secreted from the glands in the head of nurse bees, and fed to all larvae in the colony, regardless of sex or caste.

When a beehive is making new queens, the workers construct special queen cells, and the larvae in these cells are fed with copious(abounding, abundant, ample, bounteous, bountiful, liberal, plenteous, plentiful, extravagant, luxurious) amounts of Royal Jelly. This type of feeding triggers the development of the Metamorphosis of a regular Bee into a Queen Bee, including the fully developed ovaries needed for the Queen to lay up to 1500 eggs.

The Transformation of an everyday honey bee into an Amazing Queens reveals one of the most striking examples of what GOD'S **WORD** Meditated upon Daily will do in a Believers Life!

Jesus reveals this to us in the Gospel of John:

John 6:51 I am the living bread which came down from heaven: if any man eat of this bread, he shall live forever: and the bread that I will give is my flesh, which I will give for the life of the world....53 Then Jesus said unto them, Verily, verily, I say unto you, Except ye eat the flesh of the Son of man, and drink his blood, ye have no life in you. 54 Whoso eateth my flesh, and drinketh my blood, hath eternal life; and I will raise him up at the last day. 55 For my flesh is meat indeed, and my blood is drink indeed. 56 He that eateth my flesh, and drinketh my blood, dwelleth in me, and I in him. 57 As the living Father hath sent me, and I live by the Father: so he that eateth me, even he shall live by me. 58 This is that bread which came down from heaven: not as your fathers did eat manna, and are dead: he that eateth of this bread shall live forever.

A female larva destined to become a Queen is fed large quantities of **NOTHING** but **ROYAL JELLY**. This triggers an avalanche of molecular events resulting in the development of a Queen. It has been discovered that this phenomenon brings about a modification of the Bees **DNA**. The very **DNA** of the Bee that eats Nothing but **ROYAL JELLY** is almost supernaturally and miraculously changed.

Transformed by Eating Royal Jelly

The **WORD** of God gives to us Scripture after Scripture after Scripture which declares these truths. The **WORD** of God, Quickened by the Holy Ghost is our Royal Jelly. I will share with you in this book incredible times Of Transformation that I experienced as I was giving myself to nothing, NOTHING But God's **WORD** and Prayer! If I had not experienced these Visitations from God in the realm Of the Spiritual, Emotional, Physical, Financial, and Tangible Realms I'm not quite sure if I would believe the stories.

What kind of stories am I talking about? Visitations from angels! Christ Himself has appeared to me on numerous occasions! Instantaneous healing of my broken bones! Visions and Dreams so real that they literally felt like they were happening in the physical world! Divine protections to where a knife could not pierce my skin! Picking up a red-hot frying pan, with my bare hands, and it did not burn me!

In the middle of two gasoline fire's, and not one hair on my body was burned! And yet a person outside of the fire was burnt. Shot with a 12gauge shotgun, and I was not hurt! Flew a plane right through a set of Tall, Large electrical high lines. I mean my plane was transported through the high lines. A small how of $20 bills multiplied from a couple hundred to $2200 right in front of me. An empty LP gas tank kept our large church building heated for over two months until winter was over.

Story after story after story I could tell you! I have over a thousand personal testimonies that I could share with you. The majority of these testimonies I have witnesses, physical evidence that I could use to prove these experiences truly happened.

How can this be pastor Mike? I was eating **Royal Jelly**. **Royal Jelly (God's WORD)** was my daily diet from morning to night. Why did you stop? I allowed the enemy to distract me with news, weather, technology, and eventually entertainment. Believe me, as I am writing this book there is deep repentance in my heart. It is time for the Queen, The Bride of Christ to begin to eat Nothing but the Royal Jelly of Heaven.

John 6:63 It is the spirit that quickeneth; the flesh profiteth nothing: the WORDs that I speak unto you, they are spirit, and they are life.

**Psalm 39:3 My heart was hot within me,
while I was musing the fire burned:
then spake I with my tongue,**

Psalm 119:50 This is my comfort in my affliction: for thy WORD hath quickened me.

Hebrews 4:12 For the WORD of God is quick, and powerful, and sharper than any twoedged sWORD, piercing even to the dividing asunder of soul and spirit, and of the joints and marrow, and is a discerner of the thoughts and intents of the heart. 13 Neither is there any creature that is not manifest in his sight: but all things are naked and opened unto the eyes of him with whom we have to do.

Jeremiah 20:9 Then I said, I will not make mention of him, nor speak any more in his name. But his WORD was in mine heart as a burning fire shut up in my bones, and I was weary with forbearing, and I could not stay.

Jeremiah 5:14 Wherefore thus saith the Lord God of hosts, Because ye speak this WORD, behold, I will make my WORDs in thy mouth fire, and this people wood, and it shall devour them.

Jeremiah 23:29Is not my WORD like as a fire? saith the Lord; and like a hammer that breaketh the rock in pieces?

Am I Talking about Memorization?

No, I'm not talking about memorizing a bunch of scriptures. I'm talking about meditating on them, thinking on them, pondering them. At the beginning of 2015, the Lord basically said this to me: I want you to do nothing but eat Royal Jelly. He told me that his **WORD** needs to be my diet. That the Royal Jelly of His **WORD** was to become my main staple for the rest of my life.

When I heard this from the Lord, I began to pursue this reality. This went on for about three months, and God was moving in a mighty way. But the enemy came, and somehow distracted me. A little later in this book, I'll talk about distractions, and how harmful they are to our spiritual walk. The Lord said to me if our going to really get to the place to where I can use you to set multitudes of the captives free, then you have got to give yourself to nothing eat Royal Jelly.

Acts 6:1 And in those days, when the number of the disciples was multiplied, there arose a murmuring of the Grecians against the Hebrews, because their widows were neglected in the daily ministration. 2 Then the twelve called the multitude of the disciples unto them, and said, It

is not reason that we should leave the WORD of God, and serve tables. 3 Wherefore, brethren, look ye out among you seven men of honest report, full of the Holy Ghost and wisdom, whom we may appoint over this business. 4 But we will give ourselves continually to prayer, and to the ministry of the WORD.

Ephesians 5:17 Wherefore be ye not unwise, but understanding what the will of the Lord is. 18 And be not drunk with wine, wherein is excess; but be filled with the Spirit; 19 speaking to yourselves in psalms and hymns and spiritual songs, singing and making melody in your heart to the Lord; 20 giving thanks always for all things unto God and the Father in the name of our Lord Jesus Christ; 21 submitting yourselves one to another in the fear of God.

WHERE IS THE GOD OF SMITH WIGGLESWORTH?

Why would I say such a thing? What I am saying is similar to what Elisha said about Elijah.

2 Kings 2:13 He took up also the mantle of Elijah that fell from him, and went back, and stood by the bank of Jordan; 14 and he took the mantle of Elijah that fell from him, and smote the waters, and said, Where is the Lord God of Elijah? and when he also had smitten the waters, they parted hither and thither: and Elisha went over. 15 And when the sons of the prophets which were to view at Jericho saw him, they said, The spirit of Elijah doth rest on Elisha.

There is a deep hunger taking place in the lives of Holy Ghost people to see God move once again as he did in the days of Smith Wigglesworth. Not just Smith Wigglesworth, but Alexander Dowie, Mary Woodworth Etter, Dr. John G Lake, George

Transformed by Eating Royal Jelly

Whitfield, John Wesley, Charles Finney. Like St. Francis of Assisi in the early 1200s who had amazing miracles.

The question we should really be asking is why did these people have such amazing results? We know that God has not changed. He said: I am the Lord and I change not. The Scripture also declares: Jesus Christ the same yesterday, today, and forever.

I realize we can really half and puff, preach to return red and pink in the face, but that doesn't bring a move of God. When are we going to realize that the Holy Ghost is looking for men and women who have hidden God's **WORD** in their hearts? The **WORD** of God is there everything. Smith Wigglesworth was a Christian whose occupation was that of a plumber. His wife Polly taught him how to read. I ran into stories about Smith Wigglesworth back in the 1980s. I began to research his life, and up to this point, I have published 17 books about him.

What is amazing to me about Smith Wigglesworth is that he was simply a man, who got filled with the Holy Ghost, and then began a diet of nothing but God's **WORD**. Lester Sumrall, a man I knew personally, and greatly respected had personal contacts with Wigglesworth. Lester used a ministry in the church that I pastor still to this day. Actually, I was ordained to Dr. Lester Sumrall back in the mid-90s. I kept my ordination with him until he went home to be with the Lord in 1996. I love Lester, but he never attained the same level of faith and results that Smith Wigglesworth did.

Smith was not more anointed than any other believer. You see my friend it's not us who was anointed, but Christ within us. He is the anointed one. And until you see this reality you will be chasing a pot of gold at the end of the ever elusive rainbow. The Holy Ghost confirms The **WORD** of God! When we are filled with nothing but the **WORD** of God, then and only then will we experience to the same degree of miracles, signs, and wonders the way the early church did and Smith Wigglesworth.

LET US GET TO THE NITTY GRITTY!

Christian Bookstores are full of the books telling us how we can walk in the Miraculous Power of God! I know, I have read many of them. But just reading a book will not bring you into this reality. Actually, I believe that God is way more desiring For There to Be a Move of the Holy Ghost than any one of us on planet Earth at this time.

You might ask then: Why Does He Not Just Do It? It goes back to the problem He has always had. God has a problem? Yes, it's you and me! He is looking for vessels that are completely given over, surrendered, following, obeying, believing, sanctified, dead to self. Smith Wigglesworth declared that he had to die a thousand deaths before he got to a place where God could use him as a pure vessel for God's glory.

Here are just some of the Scriptures within the **WORD** of God that reveals these realities.

*The eyes of the Lord

2 Chronicles 16:8 Were not the Ethiopians and the Lubims a huge host, with very many chariots and horsemen? yet, because thou didst rely on the Lord, he delivered them into thine hand. 9 For the eyes of the Lord run to and fro throughout the whole earth, to shew himself strong in the behalf of them whose heart is perfect toward him. Herein thou hast done foolishly: therefore from henceforth, thou shalt have wars. (whose hearts are blameless toward Him)

The eye of God constantly looks across the earth in search of those who wholeheartedly love Him, serve Him, obey Him, follow Him, Trust Him, Agrees with Him, Trembles at His WORD!

Isaiah 66:2 For all those things hath mine hand made, and all those things have been, saith the Lord: but to this man will I look, even to him that is poor and of a contrite spirit, and trembleth at my WORD.

Isaiah 66:5 Hear the WORD of the Lord, ye that tremble at his WORD; Your brethren that hated you, that cast you out for my name's sake, said, Let the Lord be glorified: but he shall appear to your joy, and they shall be ashamed.

---

1 Peter 3:12 For the eyes of the Lord are over the righteous, and his ears are open unto their prayers: but the face of the Lord is against them that do evil.

Zechariah 4:10 For who hath despised the day of small things? for they shall rejoice, and shall see the plummet in the hand of Zerubbabel with those seven; they are the eyes of the Lord, which run to and fro through the whole earth.

Psalm 34:15 The eyes of the Lord are upon the righteous, and his ears are open unto their cry.

---

*Behold I stand at the door & knock

Revelation 3:19 As many as I love, I rebuke and chasten: be zealous therefore, and repent. 20 Behold, I stand at the door, and knock: if any man hear my voice, and open the door, I will come in to him, and will sup with him, and he with me. 21 To him that overcometh will I grant to sit with me in my throne, even as I also overcame, and am set down with my Father in his throne.

*Seeking those to worship God in spirit and truth

John 4:22 Ye worship ye know not what: we know what we worship: for salvation is of the Jews. 23 But the hour cometh, and now is, when the true worshippers shall worship the Father in spirit and in truth: for the Father seeketh such to worship him. 24 God is a Spirit: and they that worship him must worship him in spirit and in truth.

Acts 17:26 and hath made of one blood all nations of men for to dwell on all the face of the earth, and hath determined the times before appointed, and the bounds of their habitation; 27 that they should seek the Lord, if haply they might feel after him, and find him, though he be not far from every one of us: 28 for in him we live, and move, and have our being; as certain also of your own poets have said, For we are also his offspring.

Mark 12:33 and to love him with all the heart, and with all the understanding, and with all the soul, and with all the strength, and to love his neighbour as himself, is more than all whole burnt offerings and sacrifices. 34 And when Jesus saw that he answered discreetly, he said unto him, Thou art not far from the kingdom of God.

James 4:7 Submit yourselves therefore to God. Resist the devil, and he will flee from you. 8 Draw nigh to God, and he will draw nigh to you. Cleanse your hands, ye sinners; and purify your hearts, ye double minded. 9 Be afflicted, and mourn, and weep: let your laughter be turned to mourning, and your joy to heaviness.

*Find someone to stand in the gap

Ezekiel 22:30 And I sought for a man among them, that should make up the hedge, and stand in the gap before me for the land, that I should not destroy it: but I found none.

CHAPTER TWO

SMITH WIGGLESWORTH - A MAN OF ONE BOOK!

Smith Wigglesworth, often referred to as 'the Apostle of Faith,' was one of the early pioneers of the Pentecostal revival that occurred a century ago.

Without human refinement and education he was able to tap into the infinite resources of God to bring divine grace to multitudes.

Thousands came to Christian faith in his meetings, hundreds were healed of serious illnesses and diseases as supernatural signs followed his ministry.

A deep intimacy with his heavenly Father and an unquestioning faith in God's WORD brought spectacular results and provided an example for all true believers of the GOSPEL.

Exhortation

Smith Wigglesworth: This Is The Place Where God Will Show up!

You must come to a place of ashes, a place of helplessness, a place of wholehearted surrender where you do not refer to yourself. You have no justification of your own in regard to anything. You are prepared to be slandered, to be despised by everybody. But because of His personality in you, He reserves you for Himself because you are godly, and He sets you on high because you have known His name (Ps. 91:14). He causes you to be the fruit of His loins and to bring forth His glory so that you will no longer rest in yourself. Your confidence will be in God. Ah, it is lovely. "The Lord is the Spirit; and where the Spirit of the Lord is, there is liberty" (2 Cor. 3:17).

Born June 10th, 1859
Died March 4th, 1947

In this chapter I would like to share with you some of the quotes from Smith Wigglesworth, and his attitude about God's **WORD**. For years I have taught the congregation that there's Four Major Realities That Must Be in Our Life.
#1 God the Father #2 God the Son #3 God the Holy Ghost #4 The **WORD** of God

I believe the reason why we're not getting the results that we should is because were missing one or more these realities.

SMITH: There is one thing that God has given me from my youth up: A taste and relish for my BIBLE.

I can say before God, I have never read a book but my BIBLE, so I know nothing about books. **It seems better to me to get the book of books for food for your soul, for the strengthening of your faith and the building up of your character in God, [1Th 3.13]** so that all the time you are being changed and made meet to walk with God. **"Without faith it is impossible to please him; for** he that cometh to God must believe that he is, and that he is a rewarder of them that diligently seek him." [He 11.6]

If you had any idea how God seems to fascinate me with His **WORD**. I read and read and read, and yet there is always something so new, remarkable and blessed that I find it is true what the Scriptures says. As I get deeper into the knowledge of the Bridegroom, I hear the voice of Jesus saying,

"The Bride rejoices to hear the Bridegroom's voice."

The **WORD** is **"His Voice,"** and, as we get nearer to Jesus, we understand the principles of His mission; that He came to take out for Himself a people that they might be called **"His Bride." He came to find "a Body."** God's message to us to-night is that He is going to take out of His body a Bride unto Himself, and so I believe that while we talk about salvation there are deeper truths that God wants to show us.

It is not only to be saved, my brother, but that there is an eternal destiny awaiting us of wonderment that God has for us in the glory. I pray that we may be so interested in this evening's service that we may see, that God in His mercy has given to us this blessed revelation of how He lived, loved and had the power to say to those disciples,

SMITH QUOTES ON: GODSWORD

There are four principles we need to maintain: First, read the WORD of God. Second, consume the WORD of God until it consumes you. Third believe the WORD of God. Fourth, act on the WORD.

Transformed by Eating Royal Jelly

"The BIBLE is the **WORD** of God: supernatural in origin, eternal in duration, inexpressible in valor, infinite in scope, regenerative in power, infallible in authority, universal in interest, personal in application, inspired in totality. Read it through, write it down, pray it in, work it out, and then pass it on. Truly it is the **WORD** of God. It brings into man the personality of God; it changes the man until he becomes the epistle of God. It transforms his mind, changes his character, takes him on from grace to grace, and gives him an inheritance in the Spirit. God comes in, dwells in, walks in, talks through, and sups with him."

When the WORD and the Spirit come together, there will be the biggest move of the Holy Spirit that the world has ever seen.

"There is power in God's **WORD** to make that which does not exist appear."

Faith is the audacity that rejoices in the fact that God cannot break His own WORD!

"God's **WORD** is from everlasting to everlasting. His **WORD** cannot fail. God's **WORD** is true and when we rest in the fact of its truth what mighty results we can get. Faith never looks in the glass. Faith has a glass into which it can look. It is the glass of the perfect law of liberty.

"Whoso looketh into the perfect law of liberty, and continueth therein, he being not a forgetful hearer, but a doer of the work, this man shall be blessed in his deed." To the man who looks into this perfect law of God all darkness is removed and he sees his completeness in Christ. There is no darkness in faith. There is only darkness in nature. Darkness only exists when the natural is put in the place of the divine."

God rejoices when we manifest a faith that holds Him to His WORD.

When we all (with one heart & one faith) believe the WORD, then miracles will be manifested everywhere!

I've never read a book but my BIBLE. Better to get the Book of books as food for the soul, strengthening of faith and building of character.

"Faith is such a divine establishment of courage in you that courage sweeps you through every condition: You cannot come into the divine order, except on the line of being soaked in the WORD of God."

Read it through; write it down; pray it in; work it out; pass it on. The **WORD** of God changes a person until they become an Epistle of God.

"It seems to me better to get the Book of books for food for your soul, for the strengthening of your faith, and the building

up of your character in God, so that all the time you are being changed and made meet to walk with God."

"There is something a thousand times better than feelings, and it is the powerful **WORD** of God. There is a divine revelation within you that came when you were born from above, and this is real faith. To be born into the new kingdom is to be born into a new faith."

"The WORD of God is the food of faith."

"Great faith is the product of great fights. Great testimonies are the outcome of great tests. Great triumphs only come out of great trials."

"Faith is the audacity that rejoices in the fact that God cannot break His own WORD!"

"The living **WORD** is able to destroy Satanic forces."

"If it is in the BIBLE, it is so. It's not even to be prayed about. It's to be received and acted upon. Inactivity is a robber which steals blessings. Increase comes by action, by using what we have and know. Your life must be one of going on from faith to faith."

"All lack of faith is due to not feeding on God's **WORD**. You need it every day."

"This blessed Book brings such life and health and peace, and such an abundance that we should never be poor anymore."

"This blessed Book brings such life and health and peace, and such an abundance that we should never be poor anymore."

"Dare you, dare you spurn this glorious GOSPEL of God for spirit, soul and body? . . . This GOSPEL that brings liberty, this GOSPEL that brings souls out of bondage, this GOSPEL that brings perfect health to the body, this GOSPEL of entire salvation."

"If I read the newspaper I come out dirtier than I went in. If I read my BIBLE, I come out cleaner than I went in, and I like being clean!"

"I know that God's WORD is sufficient. One WORD from Him can change a nation. His WORD is from everlasting to everlasting. It is through the entrance of this everlasting WORD, this incorruptible seed, that we are born again, and come into this wonderful salvation. Man cannot live by bread alone, but must live by every WORD that proceeded out of the mouth of God. This is the food of faith. "Faith cometh by hearing, and hearing by the WORD of God."

"God's **WORD** is from everlasting to everlasting. His **WORD** cannot fail."

"I cannot understand God by impressions or feelings. I cannot get to know God by sentiments. I am going to know Him by His WORD."

"The **WORD** of God is supernatural in origin, eternal in duration, infinite in scope, regenerative in power & infallible in authority."

"You are always right when you have the backing of the Scriptures. You are never right if you have not a foundation in the WORD of God."

God's **WORD** is a living power, and it is to be alive in you!

"When you take up God's WORD, you get the truth. Remember, God is not a man that He should lie."

"God is everything the **WORD** says He is. We need to get acquainted with Him through His **WORD**."

"When we don't allow the WORD of God to be detracted, then comes the inspiration, the life, the activity, the glory!"

"God's plan for you is to forget the past in every way, because the future is so amazingly wonderful. Oh, the **WORD** of God is so wonderful! The **WORD** so possess me that I have no place but in God's **WORD**."

"None of you can be strong in God unless you are diligently & constantly listening to what He has to say to you through His WORD."

Wigglesworth's reply to a woman who asked for books on healing. 'I handed her my BIBLE & said: "Matthew, Mark, Luke & John' are the best"

Wigglesworth once told a woman he had a cure for sickness in his bag. When asked to show it, he says 'I opened my bag & took out my BIBLE.

"The trouble in most churches is people's murmuring. The BIBLE teaches us NOT to murmur....be above murmuring."

"My BIBLE is my heavenly bank. I find everything I want in it."

Where people are in sickness you find frequently that they are dense about Scripture.

"Beloved, if you read the Scriptures you will never find anything about the easy time. All the glories come out of hard times. And if you are really reconstructed it will be in a hard time, it won't be in a singing meeting, but at a time when you think all things are dried up, when you think there is no hope for you, and you have passed everything, then that is the time that God makes the man, when tried by fire, that God purges you, takes the dross away, and brings forth the pure gold.

Only melted gold is minted. Only moistened clay receives the mold. Only softened wax receives the seal. Only broken, contrite hearts receive the mark as the Potter turns us on His wheel, shaped and burnt to take and keep the heavenly mold, the stamp of God's pure gold."

"As you receive God'S**WORD** into your being, your whole physical being will be quickened and you will be made strong.

"It is as we feed on the WORD and meditate on the message it contains, that the Spirit of God can vitalize that which we have received, and bring forth through us the WORD of knowledge that will be as full of power and life as when He, the Spirit of God, moved upon holy men of old and gave them these inspired Scriptures."

The WORD of God is a stimulant to our faith. The Lord would have us all come into a new place of grace, that all may see us as new creatures in Christ Jesus, all the old things of the flesh done away and all things become new and all things of God.

No man that lives in sin has power

Sin makes a man weak. Sin dethrones, but purity strengthens. Temptation is not sin. The devil is a liar, and he will try to take away your peace. But we must always live in the **WORD** of God and on that SCRIPTURE which tells us, "There is therefore now no condemnation to them that are in Christ Jesus.

" If Christ condemns you not, who is he that can condemn you? Do not condemn yourself. If there is anything wrong, confess it out and then come to the blood of Jesus Christ. "If we confess our sins, He is faithful and just to forgive us our sins, and to cleanse us from all unrighteousness. If we walk in the light, as He is in the light, we have fellowship one with another, and the blood of Jesus Christ His Son cleanseth us from all sin."

You can come into a new experience in God, with all fear gone. You can live in a new realm—among the sons of God with power. "If our heart condemn us not, then have we confidence toward God. And whatsoever we ask, we receive of Him, because we keep His commandments, and do those things which are pleasing in His sight."

Smith - "When we don't allow ourselves to be taken away from the WORD of God, then comes the inspiration, the life, the activity, the glory!"

THE EXPERIENCES of SMITH WIGGLESWORTH
Born June 10th, 1859 - Died March 4th, 1947
{From the authors book: The Miracles of Smith Wigglesworth}

mighty conviction of sin

There was a young man at the meeting this particular night who had been saved the night before. He was all on fire to get others saved and purposed in his heart that every day of his life he would get someone saved. He saw this dejected hangman and began to speak to him about his soul. He brought him down to our mission and there he came under a wonderful and mighty conviction of sin. For two and a half hours he was sweating under conviction, and you could see a vapor rising from him in the cold air. At the end of two and a half hours, he was graciously saved.

I said, "Lord, tell me what to do now." The Lord said, "Don't leave him, but go home with him." I went to his house. When he saw his wife, he said, "God has saved me." The wife broke down, and she too was graciously saved. I tell you there was a difference in that home. Even the cat knew the difference.

There were two sons in that house, and one of them said to his mother, "Mother, what is happening here in our home? It has never like then this before. It is so peaceful. What is it?" She told him, "Father has been gloriously saved." Both sons were gloriously saved. I took this man with me too many special services and the power of God was on him for many days. He would give his testimony, and as he grew in grace he desired to preach the GOSPEL.

He became a powerful evangelist, and hundreds and hundreds were brought to a saving knowledge of the Lord Jesus Christ through his ministry.

The grace of God is sufficient for the vilest. He can take

the most wicked of men and make them monuments of his grace. He did this with Saul of Tarsus at the very time he was breathing out threatening's and slaughter against the disciples of the Lord. He did it with Berry, the hangman. He will do it for hundreds more in response to our cries.

Three Thousand People Crying for Mercy

Some years ago I was in Ceylon. In one place the folk complained, "Four days is not enough to be with us." "No," I said, "but it is a better than nothing." They said to me, "We are not touching the multitudes of people who are here." I said, "Can you have a meeting early in the morning, at eight o'clock?" They said they could and would if I so desired. So I said, "Tell all the mothers who want their babies to be healed to come, and all the people over seventy to come, and after that, we hope to give an address to the people to make them ready for the Baptism in the Spirit."

It would have done you good to see the four hundred mothers coming at eight o'clock in the morning with their babies, and then to see the hundred and fifty old people, with their white hair, coming to be healed. We need to have something more than smoke and huff and puff to touch the people; we need to be a burning fire for God. His ministers must be flames of fire. In those days there were thousands out to hear the **WORD** of God. I believe there were about three thousand persons crying for mercy at once that day. It was a great sight.

From that first morning on the meetings grew to such an extent that I would estimate every time some 5,000 to 6,000 gathered, and I had to preach in temperatures of 110 degrees. Then I had to pray for these people who were sick. But I can tell you, a flame of fire can do anything. Things change in the fire. This was Pentecost. But what moved me more than anything else was this: there were hundreds who tried to touch me, they were so impressed with the power of God that was present. And many testified that with the touch they were healed, It was not that there was any virtue in me—the people's faith was exercised as it was at Jerusalem when they said Peter's shadow would heal them.

Multitudes of awful sinners were healed

Police in Switzerland. There were more people night after night seeking to heal than there are attending this Convention. We were working until midnight. So many people were healed that two policemen were sent to apprehend me. They said I was doing it without credentials. The police wanted to see a wicked woman who had been healed of a rupture and was the means of bringing others to be healed. When they heard this, they said they wished all preachers did the same.

Multitudes of awful sinners were healed. A whole family (all wicked) was saved through being healed. Jesus is glorious. Surely He is the loveliest of all. Truly He was manifested to destroy the works of the devil. That Name manifests life as truly as ever it did.

Power of God was Present

Not long ago I was in a meeting, and the power of God was present in a remarkable way. I told the people that they could be healed without coming to the platform. I said that if they would rise and stand upon their feet wherever they were, I would pray, and the Lord would heal them. There was a man who put up his hands. I said, "Can't that man rise?" They said he could not, so they lifted him up. We prayed, and that man was instantly healed then and there. His ribs had been broken and were not joined, but God healed him completely.

God working in Switzerland

Everything I have seen in Switzerland has brought me to a place of brokenness before God. At Bern, I have stood in a place which has been packed with a multitude of people. I sold moved by God that I ended up weeping as I have seen the needs of the people and then God gave us victory. Hundreds have been saved by the power of God. At Neuchatel God was working marvelously and the devil worked in between, but God is greater than all the Devils and the demons combined.

At my second visit to Neuchatel the largest theater was hired, and it was packed, and God moved upon the people, and on an average 100 souls were saved each night, and many healed through God's touch, yet many did not have the Pentecostal teaching, and one man actually had meetings in opposition at places, but who Is the man who dares to put his hand on the child of God? This man also had prayer meetings to try to prevent people from going to the meetings, but they all turned to nothing but confusion. People came to be ministered to.

Power of God fell

The Holy Ghost is preparing us for some wonderful event. I feel a burning in my bones. I preached one night on Eph. 3 for 3½ hours, and so powerful was the **WORD** that the people did not seem inclined to move. I preached and prayed with the sick until 11:30 p.m. Four people brought a man who was paralyzed and blind; the power of God fell upon him, and us and he now walks and sees and is praising God. I have not been to one meeting where the power of God has not been upon us. I say this to His glory.

Greater Works than These

I was having some meetings in Belfast, and this is the rising tide of what I believe was the move of the Spirit in a certain direction, to show the greatness of that which was to follow. Night after night the Lord had led me to certain lines of truth. There was so much in it that people did not want to go home, and every night until ten o'clock we were opening up the **WORD** of God. They came to me and said: "Brother, we have been feasting and are so full we are we are about ready to burst. Don't you think it is time to call an altar service?"

I said I knew that God was working and the time would come when the altar service would be called, but we would have to get the mind of the Lord upon it. There was nothing more said. They began early in the afternoon to bring the sick people. We never had a thing said about it. The meeting came, and every seat was taken up, the window sills were filled and every nook and corner. The glory of God filled the place. It was the easiest thing in the world to preach; it came forth like a river, and the power of God rested mightily upon everyone.

There were a lot of people who had been seeking the baptism of the Holy Ghost for years. Sinners were in the meeting and sick people. What happened? God hears me say this: There was a certain moment in that meeting when every sick person was healed, every lame person was healed, and every sinner saved, and it all took place in five minutes. There comes into a meeting sometimes something we cannot understand, and it is amazing how God shows up.

Power of God was being mightily manifested

I was in Havre in France, and the power of God was mightily manifested. A Greek named Felix attended the meeting and became very zealous for God. He was very anxious to get all the Catholics he could to the meeting so that they should see that God was graciously visiting France. He found a certain bed-ridden woman who was fixed in a certain position and could not move, and he told her about the Lord healing at the meetings and that he would get me to come if she wished. She said, "My husband is a Catholic, and he would never allow anyone who was not a Catholic to see me."

She asked her husband to allow me to come and told him what Felix had told her about the power of God working in our midst. He said, "I will have no Protestant enter my house." She said, "You know the doctors cannot help me, and the priests cannot help, won't you let this man of God pray for me?" He finally consented, and I went to the house. The simplicity of this woman and her child-like faith were beautiful to see.

I showed her my oil bottle and said to her, "Here is oil. It is a symbol of the Holy Ghost. When that comes upon you, the Holy Ghost will begin to work, and the Lord will raise you up." And God did something the moment the oil fell upon her. I looked toward the window, and I saw Jesus. (I have seen Him often. There is no painting that is anywhere near like Him; no artist can ever depict the beauty of my lovely Lord.) The woman felt the power of God in her body and cried, "I'm free, my hands are free, my shoulders are free, and oh, I see Jesus! I'm free! I'm free!"

The vision vanished, and the woman sat up in bed. Her legs were still bound, and I said to her, "I'll put my hands over your legs, and you will be free entirely." And as I put my hands on those legs (they were covered with bed clothes), I looked and saw the

Lord again. She saw Him too and cried, "He's there again. I'm free! I'm free!" She rose from her bed and walked round the room praising God, and we were all in tears as we saw His wonderful works. The Lord shall raise them up when all the right conditions are met.

Immersed in the Holy Ghost

The last three months have been the greatest days of my life. I used to think if I could see such and such things happening I should be satisfied, but I have seen greater things than I ever expected to see, and I am now more hungry to see greater things yet. The great thing at conventions is to get us so immersed in God that we may see him manifest himself in signs and wonders in the name of the Lord Jesus; a place where death has taken place, and we are not our own any longer, for God has taken us. If God has taken hold of us, we will be changed by His power and might. You can depend on it; the Ethiopian will be changed. I find God has the plan to turn the world upside down, and to take us to places we have not yet been.

They began to weep

One time, on board ship, a young man came to me and asked me to take part in a sweepstake. I said to him, "I am preaching on Sunday. Will you come if I do?" He said, "No!" Later there was onboard entertainment. I said I would like to take part. It was the strangest thing for me. I said I would sing. I saw men dressed as clergymen entertaining the people with foolishness. I was troubled. I cried out to God. Then came my turn, just before the dance. A young woman came to take my book and accompany me. She was only half dressed. She said, "I can't play that!" I said, "Never worry." Then I sang, "If I could only tell you how I love Him, I am sure that you would make Him yours today!" There was no dance.

A number began to weep, and six young men gave their hearts to God in my cabin.

No man that sins has power. Sin makes a man weak. Sin dethrones, but purity strengthens. Temptation is not sin. The devil is a liar, and he will try to take away your peace. But we must always live in the **WORD** of God and on that SCRIPTURE which tells us, "There is therefore now no condemnation to them that are in Christ Jesus."

If Christ condemns you not, who is he that can condemn you? Do not condemn yourself. If there is anything wrong, confess it out and then come to the blood of Jesus Christ. "If we confess our sins, He is faithful and just to forgive us our sins, and to cleanse us from all unrighteousness. If we walk in the light, as He is in the light, we have fellowship one with another, and the blood of Jesus Christ His Son cleanseth us from all sin."

Boundless possibilities if you dare to believe.

At one time I was at a meeting in Ireland. There were many sick carried to that meeting, and helpless ones were helped there. There were many people in that place who were seeking for the Baptism of the Holy Ghost. Some of them had been seeking for years.

There were sinners there who were under mighty conviction. There came a moment when the breath of God swept through the meeting. In about ten minutes every sinner in the place was saved. Everyone who had been seeking the Holy Spirit was baptized, and every sick one was healed. God is a reality, and His power can never fail. As our faith reaches out, God will meet us and the same rain will fall. It is the same blood that cleanses, the same power, the same Holy Ghost, and the same Jesus made real through the power of the Holy Ghost. What would happen if we should believe God?

Many Were Healed

In the smaller hall, set apart for those seeking the Baptism of the Holy Ghost, I shall never forget the sight, how the people with eyes closed and hearts up-lifted to God waited. Did the Holy Spirit fall upon them? Of course, He did.

Here also many were healed. At another place, there was a young man whose body was spoiled because of sin, but the Lord is merciful to sinners. He was anointed, and when hands were laid on, the power of God went mightily over him. He said, "I am healed," but being broken down, he cried like a little child confessing his sin; at the same moment the Lord saved him. Glory to God! He went into the large hall and testified to salvation and healing.

I am healed!

During a meeting, a woman began to shout and shout. The preacher told her to be quiet, but instead she jumped up on a chair, flourishing her arms about, and crying, "I am healed! I am healed! I had cancer in my mouth, and I was unsaved; but during, the meeting, as I listened to the **WORD** of God, the Lord has saved me and healed me of cancer in my mouth." She shouts again, "I am saved! I am saved! I am healed of cancer!" She was quite beside herself. The people laughed and cried together.

CHAPTER THREE

Doc Yeager: When Jesus spoke his **WORD**s were filled with power and authority. Sickness, diseases, demons, nature, and death itself had to obey. It is by The **WORD** of God that all creation came into existence. When Jesus said: **the works that I do, so you do also,** he meant for us to do it in the same way he did! **How did he do it?**

He spoke it into existence. He declared that His Father always heard, and confirmed that which he spoke. He said that his **WORD**s were spirit and life. Christ came to make us one with him and who he was, and in all that he did.

God is diligently searching for those who will simply be in agreement with him. What happened is that when man partook of sin, he was put out of harmony with God. Jesus Christ was one with the Father, in **WORD**, deed, and action. He boldly declared that if you hear me, you hear the Father. The **WORD**s he spoke he declared were not his but the Fathers. Even the works that he did were not of him but from the Father. The last **WORD**s we hear Christ pray before he went to the garden of Gethsemane were: Father make them one with us even as we are one!

John 1:1 In the beginning was the WORD, and the WORD was with God, and the WORD was God. 2 The same was in the beginning with God. 3 All things were made by him; and without him was not anything made that was made. 4 In him was life; and the life was the light of men. 5 And the light shineth in darkness; and the darkness comprehended it not.

*John 1:14 And the WORD was made flesh, and dwelt among us, (and we beheld his glory, the glory as of the only begotten of the Father,) full of grace and truth.

*John 6:63 It is the spirit that quickeneth; the flesh profiteth nothing: the WORDs that I speak unto you, they are spirit, and they are life.

Hebrews 1:3 Who being the brightness of his glory, and the express image of his person, and upholding all things by the WORD of his power, when he had by himself purged our sins, sat down on the right hand of the Majesty on high:

*Hebrews 4:12 For the WORD of God is quick, and powerful, and sharper than any two-edged SWORD, piercing even to the dividing asunder of soul and spirit, and of the joints and marrow, and is a discerner of the thoughts and intents of the heart.

ONLY ONE POWER CAN TOTALLY TRANSFORM US

Please realize that there is only one power in this world that can transform the human soul into the very image and likeness of God. That is the inspired **WORD** of God.

*All Scripture is given by inspiration of God and is profitable for doctrine, for reproof, for correction, for instruction in righteousness that the man of God may be perfect and thoroughly furnished unto all good works.

It is God's will that we are transformed. **How**? By the renewing of our mind that we may prove what is that good, acceptable and the perfect will of God. Now, the devil can't have that, so he will endeavor to distract us in every way he can from the **power of God's WORD**. The Bible says that we have the same spirit of faith according as it is written, they believed, therefore did they speak. We also believe and therefore do we speak. Faith calls those things which be not as though they were. Or faith speaks into existence, the will of the Father.

We are saying what God wants us to say according to His will. When man committed sin, everything flipped upside down. At one time the flesh, emotions, motives, mind of man was completely dominated by the spirit of faith. But when man committed Sin the flesh took over. In most people's lives, their Flesh is in complete control. Their feelings, emotions, pain, suffering, agony, and circumstances are in the driver seat. They are operating in a spirit of unbelief!

And what's that all about? It's the **devil and satanic powers**. They are trying to get our minds off of Christ. They are trying to pull us away from the **WORD** of God. The demonic world knows that if you and I eat Royal Jelly 24 hours a day, seven days a week, 36 five days out of the year, we will literally live, walk, and moved for Jesus did in his earthly ministry.

You'll live where God lives. You'll walk with God walks. You will do what God does. Back in the Fall of 1979 to July 1981, my wife and I were pastoring a little Assemblies of God church in Three Springs Pennsylvania. We did not have a TV or read the newspaper.

Going Deeper in God

We were preparing to leave the church that we had been pastoring for two years. Because the church was bringing in new candidates for examination, they did not need me to preach the **WORD** to them any longer.

As a result, I was able to spend many hours memorizing and meditating on the Bible. A sense of great expectancy grew within my heart. The air was charged with the tangible power of God. I would walk the mountain behind our parsonage praying and meditating all day long. This continued for a number of weeks. At the time, I did not realize that I was about to step into a deeper realm of the Spirit.

Mifflin FGBMFI Holy Ghost Meeting

My wife and I were scheduled to minister at a number of meetings, and I had been invited previously to minister at the Mifflin Full Gospel Businessmen's meeting located in Belleville, Pennsylvania. We arrived right before the meeting was to start.

As I sat at a table with my wife, I remember that I felt no particular quickening of the Spirit of God on the inside whatsoever. One of the members of the organization came over and asked me if I would like to pray with some of the members before the beginning of the meeting. I consented to do so.

They were standing in a circle holding each other's hands. I simply stepped into this circle and took the hand of the man on my right and left.

The Cataracts Just Melted Away

The men began to pray, and I prayed very softly, agreeing with them. During this time of prayer, I did not perceive in my heart that I should pray aloud. When we were done praying, the man on my right, an older gentleman, stared at me. He said, "What in the world was that?"

I said to him, **"What do you mean?"**

He said it was like a **streak of lightning** came out of my hand, and up his arm, through his face. You could tell that something really radical had taken place. I told him that I had not felt anything.

That was the beginning of a wonderful, strange and unusual night. This same gentleman came to me at the end of the service, crying. He asked me to look into his eyes. I still remember to this day, his eyes were clear, glistening and filled with tears. He said to me, **"My eyes were covered in cataracts. The minute you touched me, the cataracts literally melted right off of my eyeballs!"** Thank you Jesus!

Right up to the minute before I opened my mouth I had not felt a single thing spiritually. However, the minute I began to speak at the pulpit, the river began to flow. I do not remember what I said, but I do know I was speaking under a strong influence of the Holy Ghost. Then I flowed right into the gifts of the Spirit after the teaching of the **WORD**. A very precise **WORD** of knowledge began to operate. I remember looking out over the people and beginning to call specific people out. Many of the women and men appeared to be Mennonite or Amish.

I began to point to specific people, and call them to come forward. As they came, I would tell them what it was that was going on in their bodies. When they would get within ten feet of me, (no exaggeration) they did not fall forward or backwards, but just begin to crumple like soft snow flakes to the floor. Up to that time I had never seen anything like it!

It was like they just simply, and very gently went down. As far as I know, all of them were instantly healed. I do not remember laying hands on anyone that night. The Father, Son, and Holy Ghost were in the house.

*How God anointed Jesus of Nazareth with the Holy Ghost
and with power: who went about doing good, and
healing all that were oppressed of the devil; for God
was with him (Acts 10:38).*

Her Face Hit the Concrete

We were conducting special healing meetings in Huntington, Pennsylvania, where we had rented a large conference room at Juniata College. The meeting room had a concrete floor with no carpet. After I had ministered the message I began to move in the gifts of the Spirit.

In this particular meeting I was quickened by the Spirit to have everyone stand facing the front in a long line. Quite a number of people had either been called out or wanted prayer. I specifically told the men that were standing behind these people not to brush against anyone's back. The reality of the presence of Christ was very strong. I knew that if someone brushed against these people, they would fall.

One of my coworkers accidentally brushed up against a young lady of approximately eighteen years of age. I was probably twenty feet from her. I saw the whole thing in slow motion. She began to fall forward. I went to move toward her, but I knew I could never make it in time. She fell forward with her hands at her side. I watched as her precious face slammed into the concrete floor. The minute her face hit the floor, it literally sounded like a pumpkin smashing and breaking in half and everybody gasped in horror.

I walked up to where she was laying. Even though I had been in the Spirit, my flesh was filled with trembling. I was fully expecting there to be blood. As I looked around her head I did not see any blood! I knew I had to quickly step back into the Spirit. As I did, I had total peace, so I left her lying there. I started at the end of the prayer line, working my way down, one person at a time. We saw many wonderful things that night. God set many free.

After the service I looked for this young lady. She was standing about where she had originally fallen. I walked up to her very gingerly. I almost did not want to look at her face because I was afraid of what I would see. She was shaking a little and crying. When I came around to her front I looked at her face.

To my amazement there was not one mark. In the natural there had to be some damage. We all heard her head when it hit the concrete. The room was filled with the sound of a loud thump. But here she was with not one mark on her face. I asked her what happened when she fell forward. She said that when she hit the floor it felt like as if she was falling into a bed of feathers!

And he went up unto them into the ship; and the wind ceased: and they were sore amazed in themselves beyond measure, and wondered (Mark 6:51).

A Divine Download of Revelation

Most times in our life as believers and ministers we are trying to believe God for more power, more authority, and greater manifestations. In the life of Christ, it was the opposite. There was so much power, authority, Spirit manifested in his life, he knew everything he said would happen.

When you begin to walk in this realm is very important that you tiptoe. There's been a number of times in my life when I had tapped into this realm. What I said came to pass, whether I wanted it to or not. Honestly! Let me share one such experience.

My wife and I were invited to minister at a woman's meeting in State College, Pennsylvania. On the way to this meeting, God began to supernaturally give me a message for this service. I have written over seven thousand sermon outlines through the years. Many of my sermons have come to me in dreams and visions. Numerous times I have simply preached what I saw myself speaking the night before from a dream I had received. All of these experiences are simply the quickening of the Spirit. We are all called as God's people to walk in His quickening.

The first Adam was a living soul, the second Adam is a quickening Spirit. In this experience, I saw a multifaceted diamond that filled the heavens. Remember, this all took place as I was driving. I was in two different places at once.

I was driving my car with my wife next to me, and at the same time, I was in another world. As I looked at this multifaceted diamond, every one of its facets was a marvelous dimension of God's nature and character. I was overwhelmed with God's awesomeness and marvelous, never-ending possibilities. I wish someone would have recorded that sermon that day as it just flowed forth from heaven through me.

The Woman Were Hit with a Bowling Ball

When I had finished ministering the **WORD** of God at this woman's meeting, I began to operate in a precise **WORD** of knowledge. (1981)

As I spoke forth what the Spirit of God showed me by a **WORD** of knowledge, I asked all the ladies that I had spoken to by the Spirit of the Lord to step out into the center of the room. The atmosphere was **electrified by the Power of God** to heal the sick. Approximately fifteen to twenty women (maybe more) were standing in the middle of the room waiting to be ministered to. The Spirit of God told me specifically:

"Do Not Touch Them. Simply Speak My WORD."

I heard this very strong within my inner man, and oh how I wish I had listened to the voice of God. Now, there was one woman who was standing in front of all the rest. They were lined up in such a way that it looked almost like bowling pins set up at the end of a bowling alley.

At that moment, un-crucified flesh rose up in me and I disobeyed God. I was not just going to speak to them, but I would lay my hands on each one and they would be healed, and wouldn't I be something (Me, Me, Me)! That's why God cannot use a lot of people —because they start thinking that they are something special. I reached out Oh so very gently touching the very first woman on the forehead with just the tip of my fingers. My wife was there, and she can testify to this story.

The minute I touched this precious lady she flew back violently. She was literally thrown back as if a mighty power had struck her. She hit the ladies right behind her. Every one of these ladies flew back like the first lady and slammed into the others. They all fail violently to the floor.

These precious ladies ended up on the floor lying on top of one another in less than three seconds. There were exposed legs sticking up in the air everywhere. I am ashamed to say that even some of their dresses were lifted above their waist with their undergarments exposed. When they all flew back it looked like a bowling ball slamming into the bowling pins as a strike.

At that very moment the Spirit of God spoke to me and said: because of your disobedience, not one of them had been healed. If I had obeyed God, every one of them would have been instantly delivered and healed. Now, instead of God being glorified, confusion had entered this meeting. I had misused and abused my position with God. To this day, I am ashamed that I didn't obey God that night. Just think if I would have listened to the Lord; those precious ladies would have all been healed instantly and God would have been glorified. I did apologize to those present.

My wife and I helped the ladies get back up and I told them I would like to pray for each one of them individually because they testified that none of them were healed. When you don't obey, there is a price to pay. Many ministers I think simply use the power of God to knock people down. But by faith, you need to direct that power of the spirit into their bodies to heal them. Kathleen and I prayed for each person but this time it was with what the bible calls "common faith" while before I had been operating in the gift of faith and healing.

(2 Samuel 24:10) And David's heart smote him after that he had numbered the people. And David said unto the LORD, I have sinned greatly in that I have done: and now, I beseech thee, O LORD, take away the iniquity of thy servant; for I have done very foolishly.

Bought Tickets to Germany

We were getting ready to move from the parsonage of the church we had been pastoring. As I was in prayer one morning, the Spirit of God spoke to my heart, Go to Germany! It was very strong that I needed to go to Germany. When I shared this with my wife, without hesitation she agreed. We had to raise money in order to buy the tickets and go.

We put our car on the market, and sold it within a couple of days. That was a miracle within itself. That was the Sports Granada that I had outfitted with ridiculous equipment. It was an older gentleman that bought the car. We tried to sell whatever else we could. What we could not sell, we put in storage. We then bought round-trip tickets to Frankfurt, Germany. My wife Kathleen, Michael (who was now three months old) and myself caught a plane and landed in Frankfurt, Germany.

Frankfurt Germany, Now What?

When we entered the airport terminal I did not know what else to do. This pattern is how God has led me the majority of my spiritual life. I do not try to figure out what to do—I simply take one baby step at a time. As I was standing in the terminal, simply being quiet and waiting to hear what the Spirit would say, the Spirit quickened my heart to go to the American military welcome center at the airport.

I remember walking towards the military welcome center with my wife and child. Standing right outside of the glass window office area was a gentleman who was dressed in military clothing. Because I had been in the navy and not in the army, I did not know their ranking system. This particular military man, who was an older Hispanic man, was some type of officer. I walked up to him and simply started talking. It turns out he was a sergeant, and he was stationed at the local American military base. He asked me what we were doing in Germany.

I told him that I was a minister, and how the Spirit of God quickened my heart to come to Germany to minister and that we had come by faith with no connections in the Christian community. He then informed me that he himself was a pastor and had connections throughout Germany. As I was speaking to him, God moved on his heart to help us! He also invited us to come and preach to his congregation. We had a wonderful move of God's Spirit in the church. Then the pastor helped us get the proper papers and ID's to go to any military base in Germany. The doors began to swing open for us!

And the angel of the Lord spake unto Philip, saying, Arise, and go toward the south unto the way that goeth down from Jerusalem unto Gaza, which is desert (Acts 8:26).

My Son would have Burned Alive in a Fire
Michael Would Have Burned to DEATH with Out an Open Vision!

While we were in Germany we bought a used Audi 100, with which we crisscrossed all over Germany, Holland, and the outskirts of France. One day as we were driving on the autobahn (German highway), I had an open vision.

Transformed by Eating Royal Jelly

All of a sudden, right in front of my eyes I saw the back seat of our car exploding in fire, with our son Michael burning alive in his car seat. This was a very disturbing image. I remember shaking my head, thinking this can't be! I tried to ignore it for a little while, but I had the vision again! I told my wife what I'd seen. She informed me that she was also seeing the same thing; that is why she had her chair leaning back, so she could grab Michael. She also had been praying in her heavenly tongues.

We pulled off to the side of the autobahn immediately, and got out of the car with Michael. I began to search high and low over the car. As Kathleen held Michael I searched underneath, in the trunk, and inside out but I could find nothing wrong. Not knowing what else to do, we all got back into the vehicle, strapped Michael back into his baby seat, and went back onto the autobahn. Kathee kept her seat back as far as possible, and put her hand on Michael.

As we were driving, the same vision burst in front of my eyes stronger than ever. The vision was so real that I could barely see what was in front of me. Now, without a shadow of doubt, I knew something was going on. That God was trying to save us from a terrible tragedy! At the same time my eyes began to water and burn from some nasty fumes.

This time I pulled over to the side of the road as quickly as I could. I turned off the car and we evacuated the vehicle like it was about to explode. After I had got Kathleen and Michael far enough from the vehicle, I once again began to meticulously comb the car, which again came up with nothing wrong. The last thing to try was to pull the seat out of the back.

Since all American vehicles have their back seats attached, I wasn't sure how to do it. Yet to my surprise and delight, I discovered that the backseat was removable as I grabbed it. As I pulled it out, I was instantly overwhelmed by acidic fumes. Right underneath where

Michael was sitting was a large twelve-volt battery! Acidic fumes were rolling out of its open caps at an alarming rate, bubbling and boiling. It was obvious that this battery was about to explode at any moment!

We managed to get the vehicle to a mechanic shop to be repaired. The mechanic told us that the alternator was putting out way too much amperage, perhaps due to some malfunctioning diodes.

He also informed us that had we not stopped the car, the battery would definitely have exploded into flames, and our precious little boy, Michael, would have been burned to death. Many believers die early and some from tragic deaths because they are not sensitive enough to the signs from the Spirit. They are not living within what I call the Realm of Faith and obedience.

He hath said, which heard the WORDs of God, which saw the vision of the Almighty, falling into a trance, but having his eyes open (Numbers 24:4).

God Provides an Apartment

We had been ministering in a church in the industrial part of Germany. God had moved in a wonderful way. The pastor and congregation did not realize it, but we had nowhere to go after this service. We did not have any more services lined up at the moment.

I did not tell this pastor anything about our situation. I like the opportunity to watch God work. If I would have told the people our needs or what was going on, then most likely they would have responded out of compassion to help us. But I love to live on the forefront of watching God perform perfectly-orchestrated divine events. For this reason, Kathee and I did not tell anyone what was going on.

We simply held hands together and **prayed**, asking God for somewhere to stay that night. After the meeting, a German woman in her 50's approached us very timidly. She informed us that her husband was working in Saudi Arabia for the oil industry and that she had an apartment in the area. She was leaving for Saudi Arabia the next day and was desperate for someone to stay at her apartment.

She asked us if we could possibly stay at her home until she got back within the next month. Remember, this lady had just met us and we were complete strangers to her. Not only that, but we were foreigners from America.

Kathee and I both looked at each other, knowing once again the Lord had come through for us. We told her that we would be willing to do that for her. She also encouraged us to eat all of the food that there was in her house, and we were glad to accommodate her request!

I have been young, and now am old; yet have I not seen the righteous forsaken, nor his seed begging bread (Psalms 37:25).

German Professor Hunts Us down

We continued to minister in the local area where we were staying. Eventually we had also consumed all of the food in the sister's apartment as she given us the liberty to do. All of our finances were completely depleted. We did not even have any money for gasoline.

I got up early in the morning - as per my usual routine - it was time for me to talk to God: about our needs. We were in Germany at this time, doing missionary work.

We were also completely out of food, money and gas for our car. Our one-year-old son was having to depend on mom for all of his nourishment. The apartment we were staying in, at this time, had a long hallway leading to all rooms: straight ahead was a very small front room (with sliding doors); on the right-hand was a small kitchen and on the left-hand was the bedroom.

I was in the front room praying and crying out to God. I never complain, gripe, or tell God what is wrong when I pray. Prayer, supplication, and thanksgiving are the order of the day. So, I was talking to the **Father,** in the name of **Jesus**, and I knew, that He already knew what we needed. Still, He tells us in His **WORD** to let Him know what we need.

After I was done talking to the **Father**, I stepped into the realm of praise and thanksgiving. I lifted my hands and began to dance before the Lord. My dance is not elaborate, orchestrated, symbolic or a performance. It is just me, lifting my feet (kind of kicking them around) and jumping a little bit - in a rather comical, childlike fashion. Some people really believe that they have to get into some kind of elaborate system of swinging their arms and bodies: I just keep it really simple, sincere, and from my heart.

While I was seeking God, my wife was in the kitchen, cleaning up. During me singing in tongues and dancing before the Lord, there was a knock on the apartment door, which I did not hear. My wife, however, did hear the knocking. She put down the dishes and headed for the door.

Now, as far as we were aware, no one knew where we were staying. My wife opened the door to a tall, distinguished-looking, German gentleman. He informed her that he had been looking for us. He said he'd been actually hunting us down, because God had used us in a service where he'd experienced his first supernatural encounter.

My wife came to inform me about the gentleman at the door. So, I walked down the skinny hallway, to where this gentleman was standing, to speak to him.

Transformed by Eating Royal Jelly

I did have a recollection of meeting him at a previous service; I'd prayed for him to be filled with the Holy Ghost and I remember him speaking in tongues. At the time, I had no idea of his background. He gave me quite an impressive resume of who he was; it turns out he was a professor at a local German college.

He shared with us how he had struggled to believe in the supernatural, because of his superior intellect, but when he came to the service I was ministering at, his world was turned upside down! He had experienced God! When he left that meeting, he said, the Spirit of the Lord was upon him. He also said the Lord spoke to him for the first time he could ever remember. The Lord told him specifically that he was to find me and give me a certain amount of money.

Ever since the Lord had spoken to him (a number of days previously) he had been trying to find us. He had just learned of our address from someone at a church we had been ministering at. Now ... here he was! Standing at our door, during the exact same time when I had been praying— praising and thanking God for the finances and food we needed. Before he left, he handed us an envelope. When he'd gone we opened up the envelope and it was exceedingly abundantly above all that we could ever ask or hope for. We did not have any more financial worries or needs until we left Germany.

Jesus saith unto them, Fill the waterpots with water. And they Þ lled them up to the brim. And he saith unto them, Draw out now, and bear unto the governor of the feast. And they bare it. When the ruler of the feast had tasted the water that was made wine, and knew not whence it was: (but the servants which drew the water knew;) the governor of the feast called the bridegroom (John 2:7-9).

Germans Falling Out Of Their Chairs

EVERYONE FELL To The Floor WEEPING as I Was Preaching!

I was ministering in a German-speaking church called The Industrial Center of Germany. This church was situated about five stories up in a high-rise office complex. They did not have a pastor in this church at the time. They had a board of elders, and I understood one of the men was an oil tycoon. He was the one who supported all the activities and outreaches of the church. I had an interpreter with us who was a famous German worship leader and singer.

When I preached at the church, I ministered a radical message on being one hundred percent, completely and totally sold out to Jesus Christ. I shared that there was a price to be paid to enter the deeper things of God and that you had to die to the flesh to live in the Spirit. Jesus gave His everything, and now it was our turn to give everything. About two-thirds of the way through this message, something amazing happened.

As I stood before the congregation to speak, the Holy Ghost began to move upon me in a mighty way dealing with the subject of being completely sold out 100% to Jesus Christ. The presence of God was manifested in a very strong and real way. Something amazing happened as I was about 35 to 45 minutes into my message.

All of a sudden, the **Spirit of God fell** upon that congregation in such a mighty way that everyone in that church **fell out of their chairs at once.**Instantly everyone in the congregation was on the floor weeping and wailing under the influence of the Holy Spirit.

This was such a strange occurrence because neither my interpreter or I seem to be feeling or experiencing what everybody else was. This happened in such a synchronized way that the thought came to me that for some reason they had organized this as a church.

Transformed by Eating Royal Jelly

Because I no longer had their attention, I simply quit preaching, and got down on my knees, and started praying along with them. This continued for quite a while. Eventually, the weeping and crying stopped, and people began to get up and trickle away from the meeting. **No one was talking.** There was a Holy hush upon the whole congregation. One of the leaders of the church invited us with a whisper down to the next floor where there had been a meal prepared for us in the fellowship hall.

As we sat down to eat, I could tell that they were all looking at me in a strange way. As my wife and I ate the food that was prepared to for us nobody in the room spoke at all. I finally worked up enough courage to speak to the brother who was on my left. I simply asked the man if this happened very often?

He replied, **"Does what happen very often?"**

I said, **"Where all the people suddenly as one fall on the floor and start praying, crying and weeping?**

" He looked at me as if something was wrong. **He told me they had never seen or experienced anything like this before in their church services".**

This had been a divine move of the Holy Ghost that came about as I was preaching on being completely sold out to **Jesus Christ.** The end results of this meeting were that the leadership of this church was so moved that they offered my wife and me to become their pastors. They told us that our financial needs were not to be concerned about because one of the brothers was an oil tycoon. I told them that I could not speak German, and therefore I would not make a good pastor.

They said this would be no problem because they would provide an interpreter into I became fluent in their language. I got quiet before the Lord and asked him whether I should accept this offer? The Lord very strongly spoke to my heart and said: No, I have other plans for you, and as it is not for you to pastor this church.

I informed them that I could not accept their offer, but that I was truly grateful and humbled by their request.

Prophetic WORD Flowing like a River

(2015)

I'm sleeping in bed the other night and all night long, the **WORD** of God is going through my mind like a Mighty River. Scripture after scripture just going through my mind, washing me, cleansing me, purging me.

Jesus said this would happen in the gospel of John chapter 17. He said: Sanctify Them Through Thy **WORD** For That **WORD** Is Truth. Remember the book of Ephesians says that the bride of Christ will be without spot or blemish, wrinkle or any such thing by the washing of the water of the **WORD** of God!

So I'm lying in bed when Suddenly I shifted into another dimension, into a place where the prophetic **WORD** of knowledge and wisdom is flowing like a river. all of a sudden I'm seeing people's faces who I know before my eyes while God is giving me specific **WORD**s of knowledge for these people.

All of these faces are People I know. So when I get up the next morning, I waited for a while, but then I open up my Facebook. I sent messages to all of these people privately.

I said, to Dave H.... This is what the Lord showed me last night in a dream. The same to Dan L..... This is what the Lord showed me. Then I sent a message to Johnny B..... This is what the Lord showed me. Another message to, Robert F.... and his wife. This what the Lord showed me. To Brother Clev.... This is what the Lord showed me. Person after person I contacted. After each message, I asked each person to respond by letting me know if the **WORD** I had for them was accurate? Is this God?

Everyone but one so far has responded by telling me that the **WORD**s the Lord had given me for them were right on. Everyone came back and said, Wow. The one brother said, I never even told anybody what was going on in my life. He said, Oh man, Wow, this is God.

Why Pastor Mike? How could so many **WORD**s of knowledge, and wisdom be flowing at the same time? Here's the answer: Royal Jelly. It is not because I'm praying eight hours a day in the spirit, or I am fasting three or four days a week. Do not get me wrong, prayer and fasting are important. But if you are praying and fasting without meditating upon God's **WORD** all day Long, plus not corrupting your mind with any useless info, you will get very little results.

Here is another example of when I was eating nothing but Royal jelly in about 2001.

COULD NOT MOVE or SPEAK for over 2 hours

My family and I traveled out West ministering in different churches and visiting relatives in Wisconsin. We were invited to speak at a church in Minneapolis, Minnesota. The pastor actually had two different churches that he pastored. One of these churches was in the suburbs, and the other one was in the heart of Minneapolis.

The larger of the two churches was in the suburbs. I was to minister at the larger church first, and then immediately go to his other church downtown. The whole congregation was in the same service that morning. There were approximately 140 to 160 people including women, men, children, and babies in the sanctuary.

As I began to speak, I found myself unexpectedly speaking on the subject of The year that King Uzziah died, I saw the Lord high and lifted up, and his glory filled the Temple, which is found in the book of Isaiah!

The unction of the Holy Ghost was upon me so strong, that it just flowed out of my belly like rivers of living water. To this day I do not remember everything that I said. As I was speaking, I sensed an amazing heavenly touch of God's presence on myself and on everyone in the sanctuary.

The spirit of God was on me in a mighty way, and yet I was aware of the time factor. In order to get to Pastor Bill's sister church downtown Minnesota, I was not going to have time to lay hands on or pray for anyone. If God was going to confirm his **WORD** with signs following, then he would have to do it without me being there.

It turns out that is exactly what God wanted to do! When I was at the limit of the amount of time allotted to me, I quickly closed with a prayer. I did not say anything to the pastor or anyone else as I grabbed my Bible to leave the sanctuary. My family was already loaded up and waiting for me in our vehicle. As I ran out the door I perceived something strange, awesome and wonderful was beginning to happen to the congregation. There was a heavy, amazing and holy hush that had come upon them.

By the time I arrived at the other church, their worship had already begun. As I stood up in the pulpit to Minister God's **WORD**, the Holy Spirit began to speak to me again, with a completely, totally different message. God did wonderful things in the sister church downtown that afternoon as I preached a message on being radically sold out and committed to Christ. Everyone ended up falling out of their chairs to the floor on their faces, weeping and crying before the Lord.

This is not something I have ever encouraged any congregation to do. I have seen this happen numerous times where I simply have to stop preaching because the presence of God is so strong, and so real that people cannot stay in their seats. I would stop preaching, get on my face, and just wait on God, as he moved on the people's hearts.

After that service, we went back to our fifth wheel trailer at the local campgrounds where we were camping. Later in the day, I received a phone call from this pastor. He was acting rather strange and speaking very softly in a very hushed manner.

He asked me with a whisper: does that always happen after you are done preaching? I said to him, tell me what happened. He said, "As you were headed out the door, I began to melt to the floor, I could not keep standing, and I found myself pinned to the floor of the sanctuary.

Transformed by Eating Royal Jelly

I could not move or speak." Now all the children (including babies) were in the sanctuary with the rest of the congregation. He said he personally could not move for two and a half hours. During this whole experience, he did not hear another sound in the facility. For over two and a half hours he just simply laid there not being able to move or speak a **WORD** under the presence and mighty hand of God. After two and a half hours Pastor Bill was able to finally move and to get up.

He had thought for sure that he was the only one still left in the church. Everybody must have gone home a long time ago, and that he was there by himself. But to his complete shock and amazement, everybody was still there, laying on the floor. Nobody could move or speak for over two and a half hours! Men, women, children and even the babies were still lying on the floor, not moving, talking, or crying! God was in the house! The tangible, overwhelming, solemn, presence and holiness of God had come!

Pastor Bill asked me to come over to his house so we could talk about what happened that day in his church service. My family and I arrived. He invited us inside. He asked if this normally happens wherever I went. I informed him, no, but many wonderful and strange things do take place. It did not always happen, except when I get myself in a place of complete, absolute surrender and submission to Jesus Christ.

This submission included not putting ANYTHING else but the **WORD** of God into my heart. When I simply seek the face of God, by praying, giving myself completely to the **WORD**, meditation, singing, and worship, intimacy with the Father, Son, and Holy Ghost, this was the result! God is not a respecter of people, what he does for one, he will do for others!

CHAPTER FOUR

God's **WORD** will change you. It'll change your nature. It will change your character. God's **WORD** Will change your attitude, but who's willing to do Nothing but eat and drink The **WORD** of God? I've got to do it! I have been hearing the Heavenly Father say to my heart, It Is Time!

Not only is it time for Mike Yeager to do nothing but eat and drink the knowledge of God to the Scriptures, it is time for all of His Church to do the same. I heard the Spirit of God in my heart say, it is time. It is time. It is time. God gave Smith Wigglesworth, a prophetic **WORD** about the end time revival. You can read it on the Internet.

WIGGLESWORTH on END-TIME REVIVAL:- "The WORD and the SPIRIT JOINED"

NOTE: Before we get to Wigglesworth's prophecy, it is important to understand that there have been two major types of Revival in history. Before about 1900, virtually every Revival worldwide was basically a 'Repentance' Revival - with great conviction of sin and piercing preaching at the center of it. Eg. Finney, Wesley, Whitefield, etc. But after the Welsh Revival and Azusa Street in 1904-1906, tongues and healings began to be seen in more and more Revivals.

The Hebrides Revival of 1949 was basically the last one of the "old" type that I have come across. It was the last one NOT to have a 'Pentecostal' emphasis, so to speak.

Research shows that after 1950, pretty much every major

Revival worldwide has been a "miracles, tongues and healings" type of Revival. The rise of the US 'Healing Revival' and Charismatic movement also coincided with this. God had instigated a new era.

As far as we know, all major Revivals today are of the Spirit-filled 'Pentecost' type. This has been the case for decades now. But the thing that makes Wigglesworth's 1947 prophecy so significant is this: What I believe is coming is a joining of the two types. -Piercing 'Finney'-type preaching along with miracles and healings. -Very powerful. This is probably a combination that the world has not seen since the Book of Acts.

Here is Smith Wigglesworth's prophecy (1947)

THE GREAT REVIVAL

"During the next few decades there will be three distinct moves of the Holy Spirit in the body of Christ.

The first move will affect every church that is open to receive it and will be characterised by a restoration of the baptism and gifts of the Holy Spirit. The 1st move of the Spirit ushered in the Charismatic movement – restoring the gifts and the baptism in the Spirit.

The second move of the Holy Spirit will result in people leaving historic churches and planting new churches. The 2nd move saw the emergence of the world wide House church movement – with nearly half the church splitting away from the traditional 'historic' churches to plant new ones.

In the duration of each of these moves, the people who are involved will say, 'This is the great revival.' But the Lord says, 'No, neither is this the great revival, but both are steps towards it.'

The third movement of the Holy Ghost will happen when the new church phase is almost dead. There will be evidenced in churches something that has not been seen since the book of acts: a coming together of those with an emphasis on the **WORD** of God and those with an emphasis on the moving of the Holy Ghost.

When the **WORD** and the Spirit come together, there will be the greatest movement of the Holy Spirit that any nation, and indeed, the world, has ever seen. This emphasis on the **WORD** will prepare any saint wanting to become a last days 'bride of Christ'.

When the **WORD** and the Spirit (successfully) come together then the last days revival (and outpouring of God's Spirit) will begin. It will mark the beginning of a revival that will eclipse anything that has been witnessed even the Wesleyan and the Welsh revivals of former years. The outpouring of God's Spirit will flow over from the United Kingdom to the mainland of Europe, and from there, will begin a missionary move to the ends of the earth."

— Smith Wigglesworth, 1947

According to Revival Prophecies for the British Isles, more insight on the above was to come later from one of his disciples, American evangelist Lester Sumrall (known as 'Father of Christian TV', who died 1996). Gary Carpenter's website reports Sumrall's meeting as taking place in 1939, the essence of which he reports as follows:

'Wigglesworth cried saying, "I probably won't see you again now. My job is almost finished." As he continued to pray, he cried "I see it, I see it!"

'Brother Sumrall asked, "What do you see, what do you see? He said, "I see a healing revival coming right after World War II. It'll be so easy to get people healed. I see it! I see it! I won't be here for it, but you will be." And there was a healing revival right after the war.

'He continued to prophesy, "I see another one. I see people of all different denominations being filled with the Holy Ghost." That was the Charismatic Revival. God raised up people during that era, like the Full Gospel Businessmen.

'Then Brother Wigglesworth continued, "I see another move of God. I see auditoriums full of people, coming with notebooks. There will be a wave of teaching on faith and healing." We did experience that wave he saw, and we call it the **WORD** of Faith movement.

'Then he prophesied, "After that, after the third wave," he started sobbing. "I see the last day revival that's going to usher in the precious fruit of the earth. It will be the greatest revival this world has ever seen! It's going to be a wave of the gifts of the Spirit. The ministry gifts will be flowing on this planet earth. I see hospitals being emptied out, and they will bring the sick to the churches where they allow the Holy Ghost to move".'

THE WORD ONLY CHALLENGE!

Smith Wigglesworth said the day will come when the Spirit and the **WORD** will come together and there'll be an explosion the likes that this world has never seen. The greatest power in the world is not an atom bomb. It's the **WORD** of God hidden in your heart and quickened and made alive by the Holy Ghost.

You might say, well, you know, pastor, I can't really do nothing but eat the **WORD** of God every day of my life. So I guess I won't eat the **WORD** of God anymore at all. No beloved whatever you do not stop eating the **WORD** of God simply because you're not going to make A 100% commitment to God's **WORD**.

But I'm telling you if you really want radical transformation, I mean if you really want to take off like a rocket spiritually, just do what I am sharing with you in this book and you will literally take off like a rocket.

So let's pray: father, I thank you that the **WORD** will not return void. I thank you for doing a mighty work in our hearts. I thank you, Lord, that heaven and earth will pass away, but your **WORD** will never pass away. Lord, let it become real to us now!

I quietly began to cry out to the Lord for our safe landing. I took authority over the devil and all the demonic powers behind this potential terrible tragedy. I commanded the landing gear to stay in place. There was absolutely no fear in my heart, nothing but peace, knowing now that God had put me there on purpose, not to be destroyed, but to speak his **WORD** over this situation.

Smith Wigglesworth Loved the WORD of God

I was saved when I was a boy 8 years old, and I have never lost the witness. I never went to school and so I had no chance to learn to read. When I got married, my wife taught me both to read and write, though she could never teach me to spell, but I do the best I can.

I so love the **WORD** of God I do not remember spending any time but with the **WORD**. Papers and books have no fascination for me. The **WORD** of God is my meat and my drink. I get a fresh breath from heaven every time I read it. It is full of prophetic utterances that make my soul rejoice.

Imparting the WORD

Jesus was sent from God to meet the world's need. Jesus lived to minister life by the **WORD**s He spoke. He said to Philip, "He that hath seen me hath seen the Father… the **WORD**s that I speak unto you, I speak not of myself: but the Father that dwelleth in me." I am persuaded that if we are filled with His **WORD**s of life and the Holy Ghost, and Christ is made manifest in our mortal flesh, then the Holy Ghost can really move us with His life, His **WORD**s, till as He was, so are we in the world. We are receiving our life from God, and it is always kept in tremendous activity, working in our whole nature as we live in perfect contact with God.

Jesus spoke, and everything He said must come to pass. That is the great plan. When we are filled only with the Holy Spirit, and we won't allow the **WORD** of God to be detracted by what we hear or by what we read, then comes the inspiration, then the life, then the activity, then the glory! Oh to live in it! To live in it is to be moved by it. To live in it is to be moved so that we will have God's life, God's personality in the human body.

By the grace of God I want to impart the **WORD**, and bring you into a place where you will dare to act upon the plan of the **WORD**, to so breathe life by the power of the **WORD** that it is impossible for you to go on under any circumstances without His provision. The most difficult things that come to us are to our advantage from God's side.

When we come to the place of impossibilities it is the grandest place for us to see the possibilities of God. Put this right in your mind and never forget it. You will never be of any importance to God till you venture in the impossible. God wants people on the daring line. I do not mean foolish daring. "Be filled with the Spirit," and when we are filled with the Spirit we are not so much concerned about the secondary thing. It is the first with God.

Everything of evil, everything unclean, everything Satanic in any way is an objectionable thing to God, and we are to live above it, destroy it, not to allow it to have any place. Jesus didn't let the devil answer back. We must reach the place where we will not allow anything to interfere with the plan of God. (Smith

Wigglesworth)

A Supernatural Plan

The Master dealt with a natural thing to reveal to these disciples a supernatural plan. If He spoke it would have to obey. And, God, the Holy Ghost, wants us to understand clearly that we are the mouthpiece of God and are here for His divine plan.

We may allow the natural mind to dethrone that, but in the measure we do, we won't come into the treasure which God has for us. The **WORD** of God must have first place. It must not have a second place. In any measure that we doubt the **WORD** of God, from that moment we have ceased to thrive spiritually and actively.

The **WORD** of God is not only to be looked at and read, but received as the **WORD** of God to become life right within our life.

"Thy WORD have I hid in my heart that I might not sin against thee."

TEACHINGS FROM SMITH WIGGLESWORTH!

Faith in the living WORD

Published in the Pentecostal Evangel, March 11, 1944.

Let us read together the 11th chapter of Hebrews. This is a wonderful passage. In fact, all the **WORD** of God is wonderful. It is not only wonderful, but it has power to change conditions. Any natural condition can be changed by the **WORD** of God, which contains supernatural power. In the **WORD** of God there is the breath and the very nature and power of the living God, and His power works in every person who dares to believe His **WORD**. It is as we lay hold of God's promises in simple faith, that we become partakers of the divine nature. As we receive the **WORD** of God we come in touch with the living force that makes dead things live.

In **Hebrews 12.2 we read, "Looking unto Jesus the author and finisher of our faith."** As we look unto Him we receive life, and faith springs up in our hearts. And as we continue to look unto Him, He will perfect our faith. He Himself will become the very power of our lives.

We see that when the disciples were let out of prison, the angel of the Lord said to them, **"Go, stand and speak in the temple to the people all the WORDs of this life."** The message of the GOSPEL, that Christ died for our sins, that He was buried, and that He rose again, is the **WORD** of life. There is only one Book that has life. In his **WORD** we find Him who came that we might have life, and have it more abundantly. By faith this life is imparted in to us. Drink, my beloved, drink deeply of this Source of life.

"Faith is the substance of things hoped for." Someone said to me one day, "I wouldn't believe in anything I couldn't handle and see." Everything you can handle and see is temporal and will perish with the using; but the things not seen are eternal and will not fade away. Are you taken up merely with tangible things? Or have you set your affections on things that are eternal, the things that are made real by faith? I thank God that through the knowledge of the truth of the Son of God, I have within me a greater power, a mightier working, an inward power, a vision of the truth more real than anyone can know who lives in the realm of the tangible. God manifests Himself to the person who dares to believe.

As we receive life in the new birth, and the more abundant life that Christ delights to give in the fullness of the Spirit, we have received a nature that delights to do the will of God. As we continue to believe the **WORD** of God, a well of water springs up within our hearts, this is an overwhelming spring that issues out in rivers of living water.

A spring is always better than a pump. It was a well of water, springing up, to the woman at the well, but to the person who has the Holy Ghost it is flowing rivers. Have you these flowing rivers? To be filled with the Holy Ghost is to be filled with the Godhead, who brings to us all the unlimited resources of the Father and all that the Son of God desires that we should have. As we are filled with the Spirit God will cause us to move in His authority and reign by His divine ability.

"God hath in these last days spoken unto us by His Son, whom He hath appointed heir of all things, by whom also He made the worlds."

By the Son of God, the **WORD** of God, all things were created. The things which are seen were not made of things which do appear. The Son of God created everything that is seen out of things that were not there when He spoke. I want you to see that as you receive the Son of God, as Christ dwells in your heart by faith, there is the incoming of divine ability, the power of limitless possibilities within you, and that as a result of this incoming Christ, God wants to do great things through you. If we receive and accept His Son, God brings us into son ship; and not only son ship, but joint heirship, into sharing together with Him all that the Son possesses.

Every day I live I am more and more convinced that very few who are saved by the grace of God have the right conception of how great is their authority over darkness, demons, death and every power of the enemy. It is a real joy when we realize our inheritance on this line.

I was speaking like this one day, and someone said, "I have never heard anything like this before. How many months did it take you to get that sermon?" I said, "Brother, God pressed my wife from time to time to get me to preach, and I promised her I would. I used to labor hard for a week to get something together.

Transformed by Eating Royal Jelly

I would give out my text and then sit down and say, 'I am done.' O brother, I have given up getting things up. They all come down, and the sermons that come down as He wants them. Then they go back to God, with fruitage, for the **WORD** of God declares that His **WORD** shall not return unto Him void. If you get anything worked up, it will not stay worked up very long. But when it comes down from heaven, it produces fruit, and eternal results."

The Son of God was manifested in this world to destroy the works of the devil; and it is His purpose that the sons of God should also be manifested on this present earth to destroy the works of the devil.

Do you remember the day when the Lord laid His hand on you? You said, **"I couldn't do anything but praise the Lord at that moment."** Well, that was only the beginning. Where are you today? The divine plan is that you increase until you receive the measureless fullness of God. You do not have to say, "It was wonderful when I was baptized with the Holy Ghost!" If you have to look back to the past to make me know that you are baptized, then I fear you are in a back-slidden condition. If the beginning was good, it ought to be better day by day, until everyone is fully convinced that you are filled with the fullness of God!

I don't want anything less than being full, and to be fuller and fuller until I am overflowing day by day. Do you realize that if you have been created anew and begotten again by the **WORD** of God, that there is within you the same **WORD** of power, the same light and life that the Son of God Himself had? Actually it is Jesus Christ himself living inside of you doing the works.

God wants to flow through you in marvelous power with divine utterance and grace, until your whole body is a flame of fire. God intends each soul in Pentecost to be a live wire. So many people who have been baptized with the Holy Ghost came in because there was a movement, but so many of them have become monuments, and you cannot move them.

The Baptism in the Spirit should be an ever-increasing

enlargement of grace. Jump in, stop in, and never come out; for this is the Baptism which is meant to be that we are lost in it, where you only know one thing, and that is the desire of God at all times. O Father, grant unto us a real look into the glorious liberty that Thou hast designed for the children of God who are delivered from this present evil world, separated, sanctified, and made meet for Thy use; whom Thou hast designed to be filled with all Thy fullness!

Nothing has hurt me so much as this: to see so-called believers have so much unbelief in them that it is hard to move them. **Everything is possible to them that believe.** God will not fail to fulfill His **WORD**, wherever you are. Suppose that all the people in the world did not believe, that would make no difference to God or his **WORD**. It would be the same. You cannot alter God's **WORD**. It is from everlasting to everlasting, and they who believe in it shall be like Mount Zion which cannot be moved.

God heals by the power of His **WORD**. But the most important thing is this: **Are you saved? Do you know the Lord? Are you prepared to meet God?** You may be an invalid as long as you live, but you may be saved by the power of God. You may have a strong, healthy body, but may go straight to hell because you know nothing of the grace of God and salvation. Thank God, I was saved in a moment, the moment I believed. And God will do the same for you.

The Spirit of God would have us understand there is nothing that can interfere stop us getting into God's perfect blessing except our unbelief. Unbelief is a terrible hindrance. As soon as we are willing to allow the Holy Ghost to have His way, we shall find great things will happen all the time. But oh, how much of our own human reason we have to get rid of, our carnality!

How much human planning we have to become to be divorced from! What would happen right now if everyone believed God? **I love the thought that God the Holy Ghost wants to emphasize truth**. If we will only yield ourselves to the divine plan, He is right here to do great things, and to fulfill the promise in **Joel 2.21,**

Transformed by Eating Royal Jelly

"Fear not, O land; be glad and rejoice: for the Lord will do great things."

How many of us truly believe the **WORD** of God? It is easy to quote it, but it is more important to believe it than to quote it. It is very easy for me to quote, **"Now are we the sons of God,"** but it is more important for me to know whether I am a son of God, When the Son of God was on the earth He was recognized by the people who heard Him. **"Never man spake like this man."** His **WORD** was with power, and that **WORD** came to pass.

Sometimes you have quoted, **"Greater is He that is in you, than he that is in the world,"** and you could not tell just where to find it. But, brother, is it so? Can demons remain in your presence? You have to be greater than demons. Disease cannot lodge in your body when you are in fellowship with God. You have to be greater than the disease. Can anything in the world stand against you and resist you? It needs to be a fact a reality in your heart that Greater Is **He That Is in You than He That Is in the World?**

Have faith in the fact that Christ dwells in you, and dare to act in harmony with that glorious truth. Christ said, **"Have faith in God. For verily I say unto you, That whosoever shall say unto this mountain, Be thou removed, and be thou cast into the sea; and shall not doubt in his heart, but shall believe that those things which he saith shall come to pass, he shall have whatsoever he saith."**

If you have been begotten of the **WORD** and the **WORD** is in you, the life of the Son is in you, and God wants you to fully believe this reality. He says to you, **"What things so ever ye desire, when ye pray, believe that ye receive them, and ye shall have them."**

Faith Based Upon Knowledge

Presented at 70 Victor Road, Bradford, UK. Published in Confidence,

October-December 1919

"Then said they unto Him, 'What shall we do that we might work the works of God?' Jesus answered and said unto them, 'This is the work of God: that ye believe on Him whom He hath sent.' " —John 6:28-29.

"This is the work of God that ye believe." Nothing in the world glorifies God so much as this simple rest of faith in what God's **WORD** says. Jesus said**, "My Father works hitherto, and I work."** He saw the way the Father did the works; it was on the groundwork of knowledge, faith based upon knowledge. When I know Him, there are any amount of promises I can lay a hold of and then there is no struggle, for **he that asks receives, he that seeks finds, and to him that knocks it shall be opened.**

Jesus lived to manifest God's glory in the earth, to show forth what God His Father was like, that many sons might be brought to glory.

John the Baptist came as a forerunner, testifying beforehand to the coming revelation of the Son. The Son came, and in the power of the Holy Ghost revealed faith. The living God has chosen us in the midst of His people. The power is not of us, but of God. Yes, beloved, it is the power of another within us, Jesus the Son of God. Just in the measure we are clothed, and covered, and hidden in Him, is His inner working manifested. Jesus said**, "The works that I do shall ye do also, and My Father works hitherto, and I work."**

Oh, the joy of the knowledge of it! **To know Him**. We know if we look back how God has taken us on we love to shout "Hallelujah," pressed out beyond measure by the Spirit, as He brings us face to face with reality, His blessed Holy Spirit dwelling in us and manifesting the works. I must know the sovereignty of His grace and the manifestation of His power.

Where am I? I am in Him; He is in God. The Holy Ghost, the great Revealer of the Son. **Three persons dwelling in man.** The Holy Spirit is in us to reveal the revelation of Jesus Christ to be manifest in us. **"Therefore be it known unto you He that dwells**

in God does the works." "The law of the Spirit of life having made us free from the law of sin and death."

The Spirit working in righteousness, bringing us to the place where all unbelief is dethroned, and Christ is made the Head of the Corner. "This is the Lord's doing, and it is marvelous in our eyes." It is a glorious fact, we are in God's presence, possessed by Him; we are not our own, we are clothed with Another. What for? For the deliverance of the people. Many can testify to the day and hour when they were delivered from sickness by a supernatural power.

Some would have passed away with influenza if God had not intervened, but God stepped in with a his revelation, showing us we are born from above, born by a new power, God dwelling in us superseding the old. **"If ye ask anything in My name, I will do it." Ask and receive, and your joy shall be full,** if ye dare to believe. "What shall we do that we might work the works of God? Jesus answered and said unto them, **'This is the work of God, that ye believe on Him whom He hath sent."** God is more anxious to answer than we are to ask. I am speaking of faith based upon knowledge.

A testimony

I was healed of appendicitis, and that because of the knowledge of it; faith based upon the knowledge of the experience of it. Where I have ministered to others God has met and answered according to His will. It is in our trust and our knowledge of the power of God and the knowledge that God will not fail us if we will only believe. **"Speak the WORD only, and my servant shall be healed."** Jesus said unto the centurion, **"Go thy way; as thou hast believed so be it done unto thee,"** and the servant was healed in the self-same hour.

An illustration. In one place where I was staying a young man came in telling us his sweetheart was dying; there was no hope. I said, **"Only believe."** What was it? Faith based upon knowledge. I knew that what God had done for me He could do for her. We went to the house.

Her sufferings were terrible to witness. I said, **"In the name of Jesus come out of her."** She cried, **"Mother, mother, I am well."** Then I said that the only way to make her family to believe it was to get up and get dressed. Presently she came down dressed. The doctor came in and examined her carefully. He said, "This is of God; this is the finger of God." It was faith based upon knowledge.

If I received a check for £1,000, and only knew imperfectly the character of the man that sent it, I should be careful not to trust it until it was cashed in, and cleared the bank. Jesus did great works because of His knowledge of His Father. Faith begets knowledge, fellowship, and communion. If you see imperfect faith, full of doubt, a wavering condition, it always comes of imperfect knowledge.

Jesus said, **" 'Father, I know that You hear Me always, but because of the people that stand by I said it, that they may believe that Thou has sent Me.' He cried with a loud voice, 'Lazarus, come forth.' "** **"And God wrought special miracles by the hand of Paul, so that from his body were brought unto the sick handkerchiefs or aprons, and the diseases departed from them, and the evil spirits went out of them."** For our conversation is in heaven from whence also we look for the Savior.

Who shall fashion anew the body of our humiliation that it may be conformed to the body of His glory, **according to the working whereby He is able to subdue all things unto Himself?** How God has cared for me these many years, and blessed me, giving me such a sense of His presence! When we depend upon God how wonderful He is, giving us enough and to spare for others.

Lately God has enabled me to take victory into new areas, **a living-in-Holy-Ghost attitude in a new way**. As we meet, immediately the glory falls. The Holy Ghost has the latest news from the Godhead, and has designed for us the right place at the right time. Events happen in a remarkable way. You find yourself where the need is.

There have been several mental cases lately. How difficult they are naturally, but how easy for God to deal with. One lady came, saying, "Just over the way there is a young man terribly afflicted, demented, with no rest day or night." I went with a very imperfect knowledge as to what I had to do, but in the weak places God helps our infirmities. **I rebuked the demon in the name of Jesus,** then I said, "I'll come again tomorrow." Next day when I went he was with his father in the field and quite well.

Another case. Fifty miles away there was a fine young man, twenty-five years of age. He had lost his reason, and could have no communication with his mother. He was always wandering up and down. I knew God was wanting to heal him. **I cast out the demon-power**, and heard long after he had become quite well. Thus the blessed Holy Spirit takes us on from one place to another. So many things happen, **I live in heaven on earth.** Just the other day, at Coventry, God relieved the people. Thus He takes us on, and on, and on. It's

Do not wait for inspiration if you are in need; the Holy Ghost is here, and you can have perfect deliverance as you sit in your seats.

I was taken to three persons, one in care of an attendant. As I entered the room there was a terrible quarreling, such a noise it seemed as if all the powers of hell were stirred. I had to wait for God's time. The Holy Ghost rose in me at the right time, and the three were instantly delivered. That night in our meeting they were singing praises to God. There had to be activity and testimony.

Let it be known unto you this man Christ is the same today. Which man? God's Man Who has all the glory, power and dominion. **"For He must reign, till He hath put all enemies under His feet."** When He reigns in you, you will obey, and you will know how to work in cooperation with His will, His power, His light, His life, having faith based upon his knowledge, and we know He has come. **"Ye shall receive power, the Holy Ghost coming upon you."** We are in the light and the experience of it.

Sometimes a living **WORD** comes unto me, in the presence of a need, a revelation of the Spirit to my mind, **"Thou shalt be loosed."** Loosed now? It looks like presumption to a carnal man, but God is with the man who dares to stand upon His **WORD**. I remember, for instance, a person who had not been able to smell anything for four years.

I said, **"You will smell now if you believe."** This stirred another who had not smelled for twenty years. I said, **"You will smell tonight."** She went about smelling everything, and was quite excited. The next day she gave her testimony. Another came and asked, "Was it possible for God to heal her ears?" The drums were removed. I said, **"Only believe."** She went down into the audience in great distress; others were healed but she could not hear. The next night she came again. She said, **"I am going to believe tonight."** The glory fell. The first night she came feeling; the second night she came believing.

At one place there was a man anointed for a terrible rupture. He came the next night, rose in the meeting saying, "This man is an impostor; he is deceiving the people. He told me last night I was healed; I am worse than ever today." I spoke to the evil power that held the man and rebuked it, telling the man he was indeed healed. He was a mason. The next day he testified to lifting heavy weights, and that God had completely healed him. **"By His stripes we are healed."** It was the **WORD** of God that this man was coming against, not me.

What shall we do that we might work the works of God? Jesus said, **"This is the work of God that ye believe on Him Whom He hath sent."** Anything else? Yes. **He took our infirmities, and healed all our diseases.** I myself am a marvel of healing. If I fail to glorify God, the stones would cry out.

Salvation is for all,
Healing is for all.
Baptism of the Holy Ghost is for all.

Reckon yourselves dead indeed unto sin, but alive unto God. By His grace get the victory every time. It is possible to live holy.

He breaks the power of canceled sin,
He sets the prisoner free;

His blood can make the foulest clean,
His blood avails for me.

What shall we do that we might work the works of God? "Jesus answered and said unto them, **This is the work of God, that ye believe on Him whom He hath sent."**

Love Righteousness and Hate Iniquity

No man is any good for God and never makes progress in God who does not hate sin. You are never safe. But there is a place in God where you can love righteousness and where you can hate iniquity till the **WORD** of God is a light in your bosom, quickening every fiber of your body, thrilling your whole nature.

The pure in heart see God. Believe in the heart! What a **WORD**! If I believe in my heart God says I can begin to speak, and "whatsoever" I say shall come to pass.

"Now, you believe God."

At a meeting I was holding, the Lord was working and many were being healed. A man saw what was taking place and remarked, "I'd like to try this thing." He came up for prayer and told me that his body was broken in two places.

I laid my hands on him in the name of the Lord, and said to him, "Now, you believe God." The next night he was at the meeting and he got up like a lion. He said, "I want to tell you people that this man here is deceiving you. He laid his hands on me last night for rupture in two places, but I'm not a bit better." I stopped him and said, **"You are healed, your trouble is that you won't believe it."**

He was at meeting the next night and when there was opportunity for testimony this man arose. He said, "I'm a mason by trade. Today I was working with a laborer and he had to put a big stone in place. I helped him and did not feel any pain.

I said to myself, `How have I done it?' I went away to a place where I could strip, and found that I was healed." I told the people, "Last night this man was against the **WORD** of God, but now he believes it. It is true that these signs shall follow them that believe, they shall lay hands on the sick and they shall recover. And all through the power that is in the name of Christ." It is the Spirit who has come to reveal the **WORD** of God, and to make it spirit and life to us.

Wilt thou be made whole?

Read John 5:1-24

I believe the **WORD** of God is so powerful that it can transform any and every life. There is power in God's **WORD** to make that which does not appear to appear. There is executive power in the **WORD** that proceeds from His lips. The psalmist tells us, "He sent His **WORD** and healed them" (Ps. 107:20); and do you think that **WORD** has diminished in its power? I tell you nay, but God's **WORD** can bring things to pass today as of old.

The psalmist said, "Before I was afflicted I went astray; but now have I kept Thy **WORD**." And again, "It is good for me that I have been afflicted; that I might learn Thy statutes" (Ps. 119:67, 71).

And if our afflictions will bring us to the place where we see that we cannot live by bread alone, but must partake of every **WORD** that proceeded out of the mouth of God, they will have served a blessed purpose. But I want you to realize that there is a life of purity, a life made clean through the **WORD** He has spoken, in which, through faith, you can glorify God with a body that is free from sickness, as well as with a spirit set free from the bondage of Satan.

There are thousands of people who read and study the **WORD** of God. But it is not quickened to them. The BIBLE is a dead letter except by the Spirit. The **WORD** of God can never be vital and powerful in us except by the Spirit.

The **WORD**s that Christ spoke were not just dead **WORD**s but they were spirit and life. And so it is the thought of God that a living **WORD**, a **WORD** of truth, the **WORD** of God, a supernatural **WORD** of knowledge, shall come forth from us through the power of the Spirit of God. It is the Holy Ghost who will bring forth utterances from our lips and a divine revelation of all the mind of God.

CHAPTER FIVE

Eat & Drink the WORD Of God

MOST OF THOSE WE HAVE CALLED SUCCESSFUL PASTORS ARE SIMPLY WORLDLY WISE MAN. TRUE SUCCESS IS WHEN WE SEE THE IMAGE & CHARACTER OF CHRIST BEING FORMED IN PEOPLE!

The Bible says in the last days that there is going to be a famine in the land. In my opinion, this famine has already been manifested, and it is a famine of God's **WORD** hidden in the heart of believers. Many believers do not understand God. They do not know how to trust God, or to look to God because there has been a lack of those in leadership who move in the realm of faith and the **WORD**.

Much of the modern church leaders are successful not because of faith in **Christ, and God's WORD**, but simply because they are worldly wise. Using natural, practical worldly wisdom to grow their local churches, and yet the Scripture declares that *man shall not live by bread alone, but by every WORD that proceeds out of the mouth of God.*

Transformed by Eating Royal Jelly

Proverbs 3:5-6 Trust in the Lord with all thine heart; and lean not unto thine own understanding. In all thy ways acknowledge him, and he shall direct thy paths.

If you read Hebrews 11, there is 50 events in this particular chapter. We call this chapter the Faith Hall of Fame. We need to take really a good look at these men and women, and the conditions that they were experiencing. How they responded to all of these trials, tribulations, and test.

They overcame **by faith based upon the WORD that God** had given to them. It is a faith that works by love, and when you are walking in this realm of faith you will not worry, you will not be fearful, you will not be angry, you will not be frustrated, you will not be upset, you will not be self-centered, you will not be self-serving and self-seeking, you will not be self-pleasing!

True biblical faith takes a hold of God's **WORD**, and the divine nature of **Christ,** and will not let go. When **Jesus** said that faith had made a person whole, what he was saying is your confidence in me, in my **WORD**, and your confidence in **My Father** has made you whole. So it's your faith in **these three areas** that makes all things possible. The **third step, realm, reality that must be in our life to bring deliverance** is that we must eat and drink the **WORD of God**. We must eat and drink the **WORD**s of Christ, even as the descendants of Abraham partook of the Passover Lamb.

John 6:1 After these things Jesus went over the sea of Galilee, which is the sea of Tiberias.² And a great multitude followed him because they saw his miracles which he did on them that were diseased.³ And Jesus went up into a mountain, and there he sat with his disciples.⁴ And the passover, a feast of the Jews, was nigh.'

The **Passover** is indeed the most important festival, feast day, tradition and ceremony of the Jewish people. To better comprehend exactly what the **Passover** is, we would have to step back into history and take a look in the book of Exodus when God had sent Moses to deliver the Israelites from the hands of Pharaoh.

God sent Moses to the Israelites to bring deliverance and freedom because they have been in captivity for 400 years. Of course, Moses is a typology of **Jesus Christ** who came to set us free from the slavery of sin by or through the means of us having faith in **Christ, and his WORD**. God told Pharaoh through Moses to let his people go. We all know the story how Pharaoh refused to obey God. The Lord had Moses to bring plague after plague to free the people from the hands of Pharaoh. None of these plagues convinced Pharaoh to lose God's people.

There was to be one last judgment, and It was the **Passover lamb**. This would be the final blow to Egypt which would release the children of God, by and through the **Passover** God would change the world. From that moment forward nothing would ever be the same.

As you and I receive revelation on the **Passover**, and what it means to us, our lives will never be the same. The **Passover** in the Bible is talked about specifically **73 times**. It talks about the **lamb** or the **Passover lamb one hundred times.** As a result of the Passover, the children of Israel from that day forward (if they would believe the **WORD**s of Moses) could walk in health, and receive divine healing.

Psalm 105:37 He brought them forth also with silver and gold: and there was not one feeble person among their tribes.

Exodus 15:26 And said, If thou wilt diligently hearken to the voice of the Lord thy God, and wilt do that which is right in his sight, and wilt gives ear to his commandments, and keep all his statutes, I will put none of these diseases upon thee, which I have brought upon the Egyptians: for I am the Lord that healeth thee.

Did you notice that God told Moses that everyone should go and get themselves a lamb without spot or blemish? The Lord told

Moses that if you obey me in the keeping of this celebration, it will finally set you **free from the control of the enemy**! If we as believers would do likewise, with the revelation of **Christ** our **Passover lamb**, we would truly be set free and set people free. What is the **MOST Important Step** in our preparation in setting people free?

By Eating & Drinking Jesus Christ and the WORD of God!

Hebrews 11:28 Through faith he kept the passover, and the sprinkling of blood, lest he that destroyed the firstborn should touch them.

Deliverance comes when you eat of the **Passover** using God's **WORD**, with a sincere heart of love and devotion. Of course, the **Passover lamb** is **Jesus Christ**, the only begotten Son of God. John the Baptist had a revelation of **Jesus Christ**. When he was baptizing at the river Jordan, and John saw **Jesus** walking towards him, he said: **Behold the Lamb of God Which Takes Away the Sins of the World!**

Now there were conditions that had to be met for the people to have a right to partake of the **Passover lamb**, and to protect them from the Death Angel which was going to pass through the land. Everyone must be dressed ready to leave; the **blood** had to be applied to the door post and the lintel which is symbolic of our thought life and the works of the flesh. All of the men had to be physical circumcised.

To do the **Passover** justice, we would have to look at every spiritual truths, lesson that is wrapped up in the **Passover,** which in itself would easily become a book. Suffice it to say that as we partake of the bread, the grape juice as **Jesus** commanded us, recognizing by faith that it is his body, his blood which he gave for our salvation; faith will begin to rise in our hearts for our deliverance, and the deliverance of others.

In the Garden of Gethsemane **Jesus** said to the Father: if at all possible let this cup pass from me, but not my will be done, let your will be done. The cup he was speaking about was the cup of cursing. In the old covenant, it talks about the curse placed upon sinful flesh. **Jesus Christ** became a curse for us that we might be made free from the curse of the law.[47] **All the congregation of Israel shall keep it.** Everyone that names the name of **Christ** is required to keep the **Passover**. I am not referring to the one that was observed in Exodus, but the one that **Christ** declares today.

John 6:.48 I am that bread of life.49 Your fathers did eat manna in the wilderness and are dead.50 This is the bread which cometh down from heaven, that a man may eat thereof, and not die.51 I am the living bread which came down from heaven: if any man eats of this bread, he shall live for ever: and the bread that I will give is my flesh, which I will give for the life of the world....55 For my flesh is meat indeed, and my blood is drink indeed.56 He that eateth my flesh and drinketh my blood, dwelleth in me, and I in him.57 As the living Father hath sent me, and I live by the Father: so he that eateth me, even he shall live by me.

As we have intimacy with **Christ,** we will come into oneness with **Jesus Christ and his WORD**. Now we can never over emphasize the need to apprehend and the development of our faith in **Christ**. The growing, developing and increasing of our faith is extremely important to our success in bringing the **FREEDOM** to all that me minister to. Everything that we have, everything that we partake of in **Christ** has to be done by faith. All things were created by God, by faith. God created all things by having faith in himself! Believers are those who do not trust in themselves, but we trust and faith in God.

Psalm 37:5 Commit thy way unto the Lord; trust also in him; and he shall bring it to pass.

Jesus said that at the very end of the ages, right before he came back, would be there any faith left on the earth? The faith that we are talking about is a faith that apprehends the character, nature, the mind, the heart, and the will of God. A faith that takes a hold of **Jesus Christ,** and brings the believer into a place of victory over sin, the world, the flesh, sickness, disease, infirmities, and the devil.

Faith is just like the physical muscles in your body. A lot of people are out of shape physically in America. It is not because we, they have any fewer muscles then other previous generations. We have the same muscles that our parents, grandparents, or are great-great-grandparents had. Most people are simply out of shape because they are not exercising their natural muscles. They are not eating the proper type of foods. The natural world is symbolic of what's going on in the spiritual world. People spiritually are not exercising their faith, and they are not eating the proper spiritual foods.

1 Timothy 4:8 For bodily exercise profiteth little: but godliness is profitable unto all things, having the promise of the life that now is, and of that which is to come.

Meditation upon God's WORD Brought a Revelation Of Divine Healing

As I read the scriptures and meditated upon them, something wonderful happened within my heart. A great and overwhelming sorrow took hold of me as I saw the pain and the agony that Jesus went through for my healing. In my heart and in my mind I saw that Jesus had taken my sicknesses and my diseases. I experienced great love for the Son of God and recognized the price He paid for my healing.

Then it happened … an open vision! I saw my precious Lord and Savior tied to the whipping post, the Roman soldiers striking the back of Jesus with the cat o' nine tails; the flesh and blood of my precious Savior sprinkling everything within a 10-foot radius, with each terrible strike of the soldier's whip. I wept. I knew this was done for me. To this day, when I recount this open vision, great love and sorrow still fill's my heart. Yet, I also feel great joy because I know that by the stripes of Jesus I am healed.

At that moment, something exploded within my heart: an amazing faith possessed me, with the knowledge that I no longer have to be sick! In the name of Jesus, for over forty years now, I refuse to allow what my precious Lord went through to be for nothing. I refuse to allow sickness and disease to dwell in my body, which is the temple of the Holy Ghost.

Jesus has taken my sicknesses and my diseases. No, if's, and's, or but's. No matter what it looks like, or how I feel, I know within my heart that Jesus Christ has set me free from sickness and disease. At the moment of this revelation, a wave of great anger, yes, great anger, rose up in my heart against the enemy of my Lord. The demonic world has no right to afflict me, or any other believer because Jesus took our sicknesses and bore our diseases.

I was born with terrible physical infirmities, but now I found myself speaking out loud, with authority, to my ears and commanded them to be open and normal in the name of Jesus Christ of Nazareth. I spoke to my lungs and commanded them to be healed in the name of Jesus Christ of Nazareth. Next, I commanded my sinuses to be delivered so that I could smell normal scents, in the name of Jesus Christ of Nazareth.

The minute I spoke the **WORD** of God to my physical man, my ears popped completely open! Up to that moment, I had significant hearing loss, but as I listened to Christian music playing softly (at least I thought it was!) the music became so loud that I had to turn it down. My lungs were clear and I have not experienced any lung congestion since.

Transformed by Eating Royal Jelly

I used to be so allergic to dust that my mother had to work extra hard to keep our house dust-free. I would literally end up in an oxygen tent in the hospital. From that moment, to now, dust, allergies, mold, or any such thing have never come back to torment me or cause me any problems. My sense of smell returned instantly too! I had broken my nose about four times due to fights, accidents, and rough activities and could barely smell anything.

Suddenly, I could smell a terrible odor. I tried to find out where it was coming from. I looked at my feet … I wondered if it could be them? I put my foot on a nightstand and bent over towards it. I took a big sniff and nearly fell over. Man, did my feet stink! I went straight over to the bathroom and washed them in the sink.

For over forty years, I have aggressively, violently, and persistently taken hold of my healing. I refuse to let the devil rob me of what Jesus so painfully purchased. It is mine! The devil cannot have it. The thought never even enters my mind to go and see a doctor when physical sickness attacks my body. I already have a doctor: His name is Jesus Christ of Nazareth. He is the Great Physician and He has already healed me with His stripes.

Yes, there have been times when the manifestation of my healing seemed like it would never come. There have been many times when it looked, in the natural, like I was going to die. But I know, that I know, that I know: by the stripes of Jesus I am healed. Jesus Christ is the final authority in my life when it comes to the divine will of the Father. His life and His **WORD** is the absolute voice of God pertaining to every situation. Without this revelation and foundation, the enemy will be able to easily lead you astray and destroy you.

We must let go of any traditions, philosophies, doctrines, and experiences that contradict what Jesus Christ revealed to us. We must go back to the Gospels of Matthew, Mark, Luke, and John, to rediscover who Jesus Christ really is. Furthermore, we must wholeheartedly agree with what Jesus said and did. I immediately reject any voice or teaching that contradicts Christ and His redemptive work.

John 10:3 To him the porter openeth; and the sheep hear his voice: and he calleth his own sheep by name, and leadeth them out.

John 10:27 My sheep hear my voice, and I know them, and they follow me:

John 10:4 And when he putteth forth his own sheep, he goeth before them, and the sheep follow him: for they know his voice.

Revelation 3:20 Behold, I stand at the door, and knock: if any man hear my voice, and open the door, I will come in to him, and will sup with him, and he with me.

Proverbs 8:20-21 I lead in the way of righteousness, in the midst of the paths of judgment: 21 That I may cause those that love me to inherit substance; and I will fill their treasures.

Isaiah 42:16 And I will bring the blind by a way that they knew not; I will lead them in paths that they have not known: I will make darkness light before them, and crooked things straight. These things will I do unto them, and not forsake them.

The Metamorphosis of a Caterpillar to Butterfly

Amos 3:3: Can two walk together, except they be agreed?

Faith is when you come into complete and total agreement with God, God's **WORD**, and His will. By the Spirit of God the apostle Paul said: *"be not conformed to this world: but be ye transformed, (metamorphosis) or changed, by the renewing of your mind."*

Before your mind is transformed or renewed by the **WORD** you are like a caterpillar. The number of legs and feet that a caterpillar has varies. There is a type of caterpillar that has sixteen legs and sixteen feet; which they use to hold onto anything and everything they can get their little feet around. When that caterpillar becomes a butterfly everything changes, including the number of feet and even the purpose of their feet.

All butterflies end up with SIX legs and feet. In some species, such as the Monarch, the front pair of legs remains tucked up under the body most of the time. Their legs become long and slender. Something amazing happens to their feet: within their feet are taste buds and whatever their feet touch they taste.

This prevents them from eating anything that is not good for them. This could be the equivalent to discerning which voices are of God. As caterpillars, they were willing to eat anything their little feet took hold of. Now they become very picky and selective over what they eat.

You see, the butterfly (which came from the caterpillar) now lives in a completely different world! It is no longer bound by earthly things. It no longer has feet that cling to the earth. It is free to fly above all of the worries, fears, anxieties, enemies, and circumstances of life. It can literally see into the future and where it is going. It has overcome the law of gravitation by a superior law: the law of aerodynamics. As believers, when we renew our minds and leave behind the laws of sin and death, we enter into a new world called: **The Law of the Spirit of Life in Christ Jesus!**

We need to be very picky with what we eat mentally, because whatever we place in our minds and in our hearts will determine what we are meditating upon. The scriptures say: *"as a man thinketh in his heart, so is he …" (Proverbs 23:7).*

To move in the divine power and authority of Christ you must renew your mind. You and I cannot move beyond the degree that are minds have been renewed by the **WORD** of God. Everything that is contradictory to the **WORD**, the will, and the divine nature of Jesus Christ must be dealt with. As we bring every thought captive to the obedience of Christ, our ability to be used of God will cause us to soar like an eagle. Listen to what James, the brother of Jesus, said about the renewing of the mind:

James 1:21 Wherefore lay apart all filthiness and superfluity of naughtiness, and receive with meekness the engrafted WORD, which is able to save your souls.

What if I told you that your usefulness to God equals your level of hearing and obeying the voice of Christ? Of course, the obedience that I am referring to here is a true, divine faith. A faith that will take a hold of God (like Jacob wrestling with the angel) and refuses to let go until there is a wonderful transformation in your heart and in your mind.

There are so many scriptures dealing with the renewing of the mind, and the meditation of the heart, that a whole book could easily be written on this subject. I will share a number of scriptures with you that are important to this particular chapter.

Joshua 1:8 This book of the law shall not depart out of thy

mouth; but thou shalt meditate therein day and night, that thou mayest observe to do according to all that is written therein: for then thou shalt make thy way prosperous, and then thou shalt have good success.

Psalm 1:2 But his delight is in the law of the LORD; and in his law doth he meditate day and night.

Psalm 63:6 When I remember thee upon my bed, and meditate on thee in the night watches.

Psalm 119:148 Mine eyes prevent the night watches, that I might meditate in thy WORD.

Psalm 104:34 My meditation of him shall be sweet: I will be glad in the LORD.

Psalm 119:97 O how love I thy law! it is my meditation all the day.

Psalm 119:99 I have more understanding than all my teachers: for thy testimonies are my meditation.

---

1 Timothy 4:15 Meditate upon these things; give thyself

wholly to them; that thy profiting may appear to all.

Psalm 39:3 My heart was hot within me, while I was musing the fire burned: then Spake I with my tongue,

---

2 Samuel 23:2 The Spirit of the LORD spake by me, and his WORD was in my tongue.

CHAPTER SIX

Smith Wigglesworth

ALL OF THE BIBLE!

Beloved, you cannot say that all the truth is contained in the gospels, nor in the Acts, nor in the law of Moses, nor in any one part of the BIBLE. It takes the whole of the scriptures, to contain the truth of God. The more you know of the scriptures the more you know of the mysteries of redemption. There are thousands of people who know the **WORD** of God, but it isn't quickened to them.

There is little life, though there may be any amount of go because the church bells ring. And there may be any amount of seeming religious order, but beloved, the **WORD** is a dead letter except by the Spirit, and you can only be quickened by the Spirit. So we must see that this "**WORD** of knowledge" of the **WORD** of God can never be vital and powerful in us without it is by the Spirit. As surely as anything, when the Holy Ghost gets right hold of any man, his conversation is in heaven, for our citizenship is there, our Head is there. We are not like the Romans; their head is in Rome, our Head is in heaven. When we are quickened by the Spirit we pray and sing in heavenly places.

And we must clearly see that God is all the time loosing us by the Spirit. When God gets us loose we are ready for any association. No matter what ship I travel on people are always saved on that ship. And if I go on a railroad journey I am sure there is someone saved before I get through. It isn't possible for me to live without getting people ready for dying. I believe we have to live in a new spiritual realm of grace where all our mind, our walk, and everything is in the Holy Ghost. Beloved, the Spirit alone can do this. You can never reach these attainments under any circumstances in the flesh: "Ye are not in the flesh but in the Spirit." [Ro 8.9] May God help us to see our destined position.

I say, and I will never draw it back till God shows me differently, that the child of God ought to thirst for the **WORD**. The child of God should know nothing else but the **WORD** and he should know nothing amongst men save Jesus. He can never know God through a newspaper and very little through books. You will find that books will disturb your mind and cause all kinds of ruptures in your ordinary communion. God has shown me that I dare not trust any book but the **WORD** of God.

 In fact I have never read a book but the BIBLE and I am as satisfied as possible. It is the only book, and it is the only food for the believer. "Man shall not live by bread alone, but by every **WORD** that proceeded out of the mouth of God." [Mt 4.4] And we are of his substance. We are his life. There is something in humanity that God has made for all his divine attributes, that man can receive of God and walk up and down insulated through and through by this God-indwelling presence. Ah, it is lovely! And it is all because of the **WORD** of knowledge, by the same Spirit that gave the **WORD** of wisdom.

God has no place for anybody who is not thirsty. You are unusable. The Holy Ghost has no movement in you. But the WORD of God which we receive when we are born again by the incorruptible WORD: As that WORD abides, and you don't interfere with it but nurture it, you will find it has the power to make a perfect Christ in you because it is the seed of God.

The WORD Changes the Believer

God can so change us by His **WORD** that we are altogether different day by day David knew this. He said, "Thy **WORD** hath quickened me. He sent his **WORD** and healed me." How beautiful that God can make His **WORD** abound! "I have hid thy **WORD** in my heart that I might not sin against thee."

It is absolutely infidelity and unbelief to pray about anything in the **WORD** of God. The **WORD** of God has not to be prayed about, the **WORD** of God has to be received. If you will receive the **WORD** of God, you will always be in a big place.

If you pray about the **WORD** of God the devil will be behind the whole thing. Never pray about anything which is "Thus saith the Lord." It has to be yours to build you on a new foundation of truth.

The WORDs of This Life

BIBLE Reading-Acts 5:1-20.

Notice this expression that the Lord gives of the GOSPEL message - "the **WORD**s of this life." It is the most wonderful life possible -

the life of faith in the Son of God. This is the life where God is all the time. He is round about and He is within. It is the life of many revelations and of many manifestations of God's Holy Spirit, a life in which the Lord is continually seen, known, felt and heard. It is a life without death, for "we have passed from death unto life." The very life of God has come within us. Where that life is within in its fullness, disease cannot exist. It would take me a month to tell out what there is in this wonderful life. Everyone can go in and possess and be possessed by this life.

It is possible for you to be within the vicinity of this life and yet miss it. It is possible for you to be in a place where God is pouring out His Spirit and yet miss the blessing that God is so willing to bestow. It all comes through shortness of revelation and through a misunderstanding of the infinite grace of God, and of the "God of all grace," who is willing to give to all who will reach out the hand of faith. This life that He freely bestows is a gift. Some think they have to earn it and they miss the whole thing. Oh, for a simple faith to receive all that God so lavishly offers. You can never be ordinary from the day you receive this life from above. You become extraordinary, filled with the extraordinary power of our extraordinary God.

Ananias and Sapphira were in this thing and yet they missed it. They thought that possibly the thing might fail. So they wanted to have a reserve for themselves in case it did turn out to be a failure. They were in the wonderful revival that God gave to the early church and yet they missed it. There are many people like them today who make vows to God in times of a great crisis in their lives. But they fail to keep their vows and in the end they become spiritually bankrupt.

Blessed is the man who will swear to his own hurt and change not; who keeps the vow he has made to God; who is willing to lay his all at God's feet. The man who does this never becomes a lean soul. God has promised to "make fat his bones." There is no dry place for such a man; he is always fat and flourishing, and he becomes stronger and stronger. It pays to trust God with all and to make no reservation.

Transformed by Eating Royal Jelly

I wish I could make you see how great a God we have. Ananias and Sapphira were really doubting God and were questioning whether this work that He had begun would go through. They wanted to get some glory for selling their property, but because of their lack of faith they kept back part of the price in reserve in case the work of God should fail.

Many are doubting whether this Pentecostal revival will go through. Do you think this Pentecostal work will stop? Never. For fifteen years I have been in constant revival and I am sure that it will never stop. When George Stephenson made his first engine he took his sister Mary to see it. She looked at it and said to her brother, "George, it'll never go." He said to her, "Get in, Mary." She said again, "It'll never go." He said to her, "We'll see, you get in." Mary at last got in-the whistle blew, there was a puff and a rattle, and the engine started off. Then Mary cried out, "George, it'll never stop! It'll never stop!"

People are looking on at this Pentecostal revival and they are very critical and they are saying, "It'll never go;" but when they are induced to come into the work, they one and all say, "It'll never stop." This revival of God is sweeping on and on and there is no stopping the current of life, of love, of inspiration, and of power.

(Interpretation; It is the living **WORD** who has brought this. It is the Lamb in the midst, the same yesterday, today and forever.)

God has brought unlimited resources for everyone. Do not doubt. Hear with the ear of faith. God is in the midst. See that it is God who bath set forth that which you see and hear today.

I want you to see that in the early church, controlled by the power of the Holy Ghost, it was not possible for a lie to exist. The moment it came into the church, there was instant death. And as the power of the Holy Ghost increases in these days of the Latter Rain, it will be impossible for any man to remain in our midst with a lying spirit. God will purify the church; the **WORD** of God will be in such power in healing and other spiritual manifestations, that great fear will be upon all those who see the same.

It seems to the natural mind a small thing for Ananias and Sapphira to want to have a little to fail back on; but I want to tell you that you can please God, and you can get things from God, only ova the line of a living faith. God never fails. God never can fail.

When I was in Bergen, Norway, there came to the meeting a young woman who was employed at the hospital as a nurse. A big cancer had developed on her nose, and the nose was enlarged and had become black and greatly inflamed. She came out for prayer and I said to her, "What is your condition?" She said, "I dare not touch my nose, it gives me so much pain."

I said to all the people, "I want you to look at this nurse and notice her terrible condition. I believe that our God is merciful and that He is faithful, and that He will bring to naught this condition that the devil has brought about. I am going to curse this disease in the all-powerful name of Jesus. The pain will go. I believe God will give us an exhibition of His grace and I will ask this young woman to come to the meeting tomorrow night and declare what God has done for her."

Oh, the awfulness of sin! Oh, the awfulness of the power of sin! Oh, the awfulness of the consequences of the fall! When I see a cancer I always know it is an evil spirit. I can never believe it is otherwise. The same with tumors. Can this be the work of God? God help me to show you that this is the work of the devil, and to show you the way out.

I do not condemn people that sin. I don't scold people. I know what is back of the sin. I know that Satan is always going about as a roaring lion, seeking whom he may devour. I always remember the patience and love of the Lord Jesus Christ. When they brought to Him a woman that they had taken in adultery, telling Him that they had caught her in the very act, He simply stooped down and wrote on the ground.

Then He quietly said, "He that is without sin among you, let him cast the first stone." I have never seen a man without sin. "All have sinned and come short of the glory of God." But I read in this blessed GOSPEL message that God bath laid upon Jesus the iniquity of us all; so, when I see an evil condition, I feel that I must stand in my office and rebuke the condition.

I laid my hands on the nose of that suffering nurse and cursed the evil power that was causing her so much distress. The next night the place was packed and the people were jammed together, so that it seemed that there was not room for one more to come into that house. How God's rain fell upon us. How good God is, so full of grace and so full of love. I saw the nurse in the audience and I asked her to come forward. She came and showed everyone what God had done. He had perfectly healed her. Oh, I tell you He is just the same Jesus. He is just the same today. All things are possible if you dare to trust God.

When the power of God came so mightily upon the early church, even in the death of Ananias and Sapphira, great fear came upon all the people. And when we are in the presence of God, when God is working mightily in our midst, there comes a great fear, a reverence, a holiness of life, a purity that fears to displease God. We read that no man durst join them, but God added to the church such as should be saved. I would rather have God add to our Pentecostal church than have all the town join it. God added daily to His own church.

The next thing that happened was that people became so assured that God was working that they knew that anything would be possible, and they brought their sick into the streets and laid them on beds and couches, that at least the shadow of Peter passing by might overshadow them. Multitudes of sick people and those oppressed with evil spirits were brought to the apostles and God healed them every one. I do not believe that it was the shadow of Peter that healed, but the power of God was mightily present and the faith of the people was so aroused that they joined with one heart to believe God. God will always meet people on the line of faith.

God's tide is rising all over the earth. I had been preaching at Stavanger in Norway, and was very tired and wanted a few hours rest. I went to my next appointment, arriving at about 9:30 in the morning. My first meeting was to be at night. I said to my interpreter, "After we have had something to eat, let us go down to the fjords." We spent three or four hours down by the sea and at about 4:30 returned. We found the end of the street, which has a narrow entrance, just filled with autos, wagons, etc., containing invalids and sick people of every kind.

I went up to the house and was told that the house was full of sick people. It reminded me of the scene described in the fifth chapter of Acts. I began praying for the people in the street and God began to heal the people. How wonderfully He healed those people who were in the house. We sat down for a lunch and the telephone bell rang and someone at the other end was saying, "What shall we do? The town hall is already full; the police cannot control things."

In that little Norwegian town the people were jammed together, and oh, how the power of God fell upon us. A cry went up from every one, "Isn't this the revival?"

Revival is coming. The breath of the Almighty is coming. The breath of God shows up every defect, and as it comes flowing in like a river, everybody will need a fresh anointing, a fresh cleansing of the blood. You can depend upon it that that breath is upon us.

At one time I was at a meeting in Ireland. There were many sick carried to that meeting and helpless ones were helped there. There were many people in that place who were seeking for the Baptism of the Holy Ghost. Some of them had been seeking for years. There were sinners there who were under mighty conviction. There came a moment when the breath of God swept through the meeting.

In about ten minutes every sinner in the place was saved. Everyone who had been seeking the Holy Spirit was baptized, and every sick one was healed. God is a reality and His power can never fail. As our faith reaches out, God will meet us and the same rain will fall. It is the same blood that cleanseth, the same power, the same Holy Ghost, and the same Jesus made real through the power of the Holy Ghost! What would happen if we should believe God?

Transformed by Eating Royal Jelly

Right now the precious blood of the Lord Jesus Christ is efficacious to cleanse your heart and bring this life, this wonderful life of God, within you. The blood will make you every whit whole if you dare believe. The BIBLE is full of entreaty for you to come and partake and receive the grace, the power, the strength, the righteousness, and the full redemption of Jesus Christ. He never fails to hear when we believe.

At one place where I was, a lame man was brought to me who had been in bed for two years, with no hope of recovery. He was brought thirty miles to the meeting, and he came up on crutches to be prayed for. His boy was also afflicted in the knees and they had four crutches between the two of them. The man's face was filled with torture. There is healing virtue in the Lord and He never fails to heal when we believe.

In the name of Jesus-that name so full of virtue-I put my hand down that leg that was so diseased. The man threw down his crutches and all were astonished as they saw him walking up and down without aid. The little boy called out to his father, "Papa, me; papa, me, me, me!" The little boy who was withered in both knees wanted a like touch. And the same Jesus was there to bring a real deliverance for the little captive. He was completely healed.

These were legs that were touched. If God will stretch out His mighty power to loose afflicted legs, what mercy will He extend to that soul of yours that must exist forever? Hear the Lord say, "The Spirit of the Lord is upon me, because be hath anointed me to preach the GOSPEL to the poor; he hath sent me to heal the broken hearted, to preach deliverance to the captive, and recovering of sight to the blind, to set at liberty them that are bruised."

He invites you, "Come unto me, all ye that labor and are heavy laden, and I will give you rest." God is willing in His great mercy to touch thy limbs with His mighty vital power, and if He is willing to do this, how much more anxious is He to deliver thee from the power of Satan and to make thee a child of the King. How much more necessary it is for you to be healed of your soul sickness than of your bodily ailments. And God is willing to give the double cure.

I was passing through the city of London one time, and Mr. Mundell, the secretary of the Pentecostal Missionary Union, learned that I was there. He arranged for me to meet him at a certain place at 3:30 p. m. I was to meet a certain boy whose father and mother lived in the city of Salisbury. They had sent this young man to London to take care of their business. He had been a leader in Sunday school work but he had been betrayed and had fallen. Sin is awful and the wages of sin is death. But there is another side-the gift of God is eternal life.

This young man was in great distress; he had contracted a horrible disease and feared to tell anyone. There was nothing but death ahead for him. When the father and mother got to know of his condition they suffered inexpressible grief.

When we got to the house, Brother Mundell suggested, that we get down to prayer. I said, "God does not say so, we are not going to pray yet. I want to quote a scripture, `Fools, because of their transgression, and because of their iniquities, are afflicted: their soul abhorreth all manner of meat; and they draw near unto the gates of death.'' The young man cried out, "I am that fool." He broke down and told us the story of his fall. Oh, if men would only repent, and confess their sins, how God would stretch out His hand to heal and to save. The moment that young man repented, a great abscess burst, and God sent virtue into his life, giving him a mighty deliverance.

God is gracious and not willing that any should perish. How many are willing to make a clean breast of their sins ? I tell you that the moment you do this, God will open heaven. It is an easy thing for Him to save your soul and heal your disease if you will but come and shelter today in the secret place of the Most High. He will satisfy you with long life and show you His salvation. In His presence there is fullness of joy, at His right hand there are pleasures forevermore. There is full redemption for all through the precious blood of the Son of God.

Faith In God's WORD!

Transformed by Eating Royal Jelly

Published in the Pentecostal Evangel, June 15, 1935.

In Romans 4:16 we read, "It is of faith, that it might be by grace," meaning that we can open the door and God will come in. What will happen if we really open the door by faith? God is greater than our thoughts. He puts it to us, "Exceeding abundantly above all that we ask or think." When we ask a lot, God says "more." Are we ready for the "more"? And then the "much more"? We may be, or we may miss it.

We may be so endued by the Spirit of the Lord in the morning that it shall be a tonic for the whole day. God can so thrill us with new life that nothing ordinary or small will satisfy us after that. There is a great place for us in God where we won't be satisfied with small things. We won't have any satisfaction unless the fire falls, and whenever we pray we will have the assurance that what we have prayed for is going to follow the moment we open our mouth. Oh this praying in the Spirit! This great plan of God for us! In a moment we can go right in. In where? Into His will. Then all things will be well.

You can't get anything asleep these days. The world is always awake, and we should always be awake to what God has for us. Awake to take! Awake to hold it after we get it! How much can you take? We know that God is more willing to give than we are to receive. How shall we dare to be asleep when the Spirit commands us to take everything on the table. It is the greatest banquet that ever was and ever will be—the table where all you take only leaves more behind. A fullness that cannot be exhausted! How many are prepared for a lot?

"And Jesus entered into Jerusalem, and into the temple: and when he had looked round about upon all things, and now the eventide was come, he went out unto Bethany with the twelve. And on the morrow, when they were come from Bethany, he was hungry: and seeing a fig tree afar off having leaves, he came, if haply he might find anything thereon: and when he came to it, he found nothing but leaves; for the time of figs was not yet. And Jesus answered and said, No man eat fruit of thee hereafter for

ever. And his disciples heard it." Mark 11:11-14.

Jesus was sent from God to meet the world's need. Jesus lived to minister life by the **WORD**s He spoke. He said to Philip, "He that hath seen me hath seen the Father… the **WORD**s that I speak unto you, I speak not of myself: but the Father that dwelleth in me." I am persuaded that if we are filled with His **WORD**s of life and the Holy Ghost, and Christ is made manifest in our mortal flesh, then the Holy Ghost can really move us with His life, His **WORD**s, till as He was, so are we in the world. We are receiving our life from God, and it is always kept in tremendous activity, working in our whole nature as we live in perfect contact with God.

Jesus spoke, and everything He said must come to pass. That is the great plan. When we are filled only with the Holy Spirit, and we won't allow the **WORD** of God to be detracted by what we hear or by what we read, then comes the inspiration, then the life, then the activity, then the glory! Oh to live in it! To live in it is to be moved by it. To live in it is to be moved so that we will have God's life, God's personality in the human body.

By the grace of God I want to impart the **WORD**, and bring you into a place where you will dare to act upon the plan of the **WORD**, to so breathe life by the power of the **WORD** that it is impossible for you to go on under any circumstances without His provision. The most difficult things that come to us are to our advantage from God's side.

When we come to the place of impossibilities it is the grandest place for us to see the possibilities of God. Put this right in your mind and never forget it. You will never be of any importance to God till you venture in the impossible. God wants people on the daring line. I do not mean foolish daring. "Be filled with the Spirit," and when we are filled with the Spirit we are not so much concerned about the secondary thing. It is the first with God.

Everything of evil, everything unclean, everything Satanic in any way is an objectionable thing to God, and we are to live above it, destroy it, not to allow it to have any place. Jesus didn't let the devil answer back. We must reach the place where we will not allow anything to interfere with the plan of God.

Jesus and His disciples came to the tree. It looked beautiful. It had the appearance of fruit, but when He came to it He found nothing but leaves. He was very disappointed. Looking at the tree, He spoke to it: Here is shown forth His destructive power, **"No man eat fruit of thee hereafter forever."** The next day they were passing by the same way and the disciples saw the tree **"dried up from the roots."** They said to Jesus, **"Behold, the fig tree which thou cursedst is withered away."** And Jesus said, **"Have faith in God."**

There isn't a person that has ever seen a tree dried from the root. Trees always show the first signs of death right at the top. But the Master had spoken. The Master dealt with a natural thing to reveal to these disciples a supernatural plan. If He spoke it would have to obey. And, God, the Holy Ghost, wants us to understand clearly that we are the mouthpiece of God and are here for His divine plan.

We may allow the natural mind to dethrone that, but in the measure we do, we won't come into the treasure which God has for us. The **WORD** of God must have first place. It must not have a second place. In any measure that we doubt the **WORD** of God, from that moment we have ceased to thrive spiritually and actively. The **WORD** of God is not only to be looked at and read, but received as the **WORD** of God to become life right within our life. "Thy **WORD** have I hid in my heart that I might not sin against thee."

"I give unto you power… over all the power of the enemy." Luke 10:19. There it is. We can accept or reject it. I accept and believe it. It is a **WORD** beyond all human calculation: **"Have faith in God."** These disciples were in the Master's school They were the men who were to turn the world upside down. As we receive the **WORD** we will never be the same; if we dare to act as the **WORD** goes forth and not be afraid, then God will honor us. "The Lord of hosts is with us; the God of Jacob is our refuge." Jacob was the weakest of all, in any way you like to take it. He is the God of Jacob, and He is our God. So we may likewise have our names changed to Israel.

As the Lord Jesus injected this wonderful **WORD**, "Have faith in God," into the disciples, He began to show how it was to be. Looking around about Him He saw the mountains, and He began to bring a practical application. A truth means nothing unless it moves us. We can have our minds filled a thousand times, but it must get into our hearts if there are to be any results. All inspiration is in the heart. All compassion is in the heart.

Looking at the mountains He said, "Shall not doubt in his heart." That is the barometer. You know exactly where you are. The man knows when he prays. If his heart is right how it leaps. No man is any good for God and never makes progress in God who does not hate sin. You are never safe. But there is a place in God where you can love righteousness and where you can hate iniquity till the **WORD** of God is a light in your bosom, quickening every fiber of your body, thrilling your whole nature. The pure in heart see God. Believe in the heart! What a **WORD**! If I believe in my heart God says I can begin to speak, and "whatsoever" I say shall come to pass.

Here is an act of believing in the heart. I was called to Halifax, England, to pray for a lady missionary. I found it an urgent call. I could see there was an absence of faith, and I could see there was death: Death is a terrible thing, and God wants to keep us alive. I know it is appointed unto man once to die, but I believe in a rapturous death. I said to the woman, "How are you?" She said, "I have faith," in a very weak tone of voice. "Faith? Why you are dying? Brother Walshaw, is she dying?" "Yes." "Nurse, is she dying?" "Yes." To a friend standing by, "Is she dying?" "Yes."

Now I believe there is something in a heart that is against defeat, and this is the faith which God hath given to us. I said to her, "In the name of Jesus, now believe and you'll live." She said, "I believe," and God sent life from her head to her feet. They dressed her and she lived.

Transformed by Eating Royal Jelly

"Have faith." It isn't saying you have faith. It is he that believeth in his heart. It is a grasping of the eternal God. Faith is God in the human vessel. "This is the victory that overcomes the world, even our faith." 1 John 5:4. He that believeth overcomes the world. "Faith cometh by hearing, and hearing by the **WORD** of God." He that believeth in his heart! Can you imagine anything easier than that?

He that believeth in his heart! What is the process? Death! No one can live who believes in his heart. He dies to everything worldly. He that loves the world is not of God. You can measure the whole thing up, and examine yourself to see if you have faith. Faith is a life. Faith enables you to lay hold of that which is and get it out of the way for God to bring in something that is not.

Just before I left home I was in Norway. A woman wrote to me from England saying she had been operated on for cancer three years before, but that it was now coming back. She was living in constant dread of the whole thing as the operation was so painful. Would it be possible to see me when I returned to England? I wrote that I would be passing through London on the 20th of June last year.

If she would like to meet me at the hotel I would pray for her. She replied that she would be going to London to be there to meet me. When I met this woman I saw she was in great pain, and I have great sympathy for people who have tried to get relief and have failed. If you preachers lose your compassion you can stop preaching, for it won't be any good. You will only be successful as a preacher as you let your heart become filled with the compassion of Jesus.

As soon as I saw her I entered into the state of her mind. I saw how distressed she was. She came to me in a mournful spirit, and her whole face was downcast. I said to her, "There are two things going to happen today. One is that you are to know that you are sayed." "Oh, if I could only know I was saved," she said. "There is another thing. You have to go out of this hotel without a pain, without a trace of the cancer."

Then I began with the **WORD**. Oh this wonderful **WORD**! We do not have to go up to bring Him down; neither do we have to go down to bring Him up. **"The WORD is nigh thee, even in thy mouth, and in thy heart: that is, the WORD of faith, which we preach." Romans 10:8**. I said, **"Believe that He took your sins when He died at the cross.**

Believe that when He was buried, it was for you. Believe that when He arose, it was for you. And now at God's right hand He is sitting for you. If you can believe in your heart and confess with your mouth, you shall be saved." She looked at me saying, "Oh, it is going all through my body. I know I am saved now. If He comes today, I'll go. How I have dreaded, the thought of His coming all my life! But if He comes today, I know I shall be ready."

The first thing was finished. Now for the second. I laid my hands upon her in the name of Jesus, believing in my heart that I could say what I wanted and it should be done. I said, "In the name of Jesus, I cast this out." She jumped up. "Two things have happened," she said. "I am saved and now the cancer is gone."

Faith will stand amid the wrecks of time,
Faith unto eternal glories climb;
Only count the promise true,
And the Lord will stand by you—
Faith will win the victory every time!

So many people have nervous trouble. I'll tell you how to get rid of your nervous trouble. I have something in my bag, one dose of which will cure you. "I am the Lord that healeth thee." How this wonderful **WORD** of God changes the situation. "Perfect love casteth out fear." "There is no fear in love." I have tested that so often, casting out the whole condition of fear and the whole situation has been changed. We have a big God, only He has to be absolutely and only trusted. The people who really do believe God are strong, and "he that hath clean hands shall be stronger and stronger."

Transformed by Eating Royal Jelly

At the close of a certain meeting a man said to me, "You have helped everybody but me. I wish you would help me." "What's the trouble with you?" "I cannot sleep because of nervous trouble. My wife says she has not known me to have a full night's sleep for three years. I am just shattered." Anybody could tell he was. I put my hands upon him and said, "Brother I believe in my heart.

Go home and sleep in the name of Jesus." "I can't sleep." "Go home and sleep in the name of Jesus." "I can't sleep." The lights were being put out, and I took the man by the coat collar and said, "Don't talk to me anymore." That was sufficient. He went after that, When he got home his mother and wife said to him, "What has happened?" "Nothing. He helped everybody but me." "Surely he said something to you." "He told me to come home and sleep in the name of Jesus, but you know I can't sleep in anything."

His wife urged him to do what I had said, and he had scarcely got his head on the pillow before the Lord put him to sleep. The next morning he was still asleep. The next morning he was still asleep. She began to make a noise in the bedroom to awaken him, but he did not waken. Sunday morning he was still asleep. She did what every good wife would do. She decided to make a good Sunday dinner, and then awaken him. After the dinner was prepared she went up to him and put her hand on his shoulder and shook him, saying, "Are you never going to wake up?" From that night that man never had any more nervousness.

A man came to me for whom I prayed. Then I asked, "Are you sure you are perfectly healed?" "Well," he said, "there is just a little pain in my shoulder." "Do you know what that is?" I asked him. "That is unbelief. Were you saved before you believed or after?" "After." "You will be healed after." "It is all right now," he said, It was all right before, but he hadn't believed.

The WORD of God is for us. It is by faith that it might be by grace.!

CHAPTER SEVEN

A Woman Fell At My Feet Weeping!

If you really want to hear the still small voice of God, then you need to take the time that is necessary to meditate upon the scriptures. As you meditate upon the written **WORD**, the Holy Spirit will be able to speak to you in a much clearer way.

Through the years, I have operated in the **WORD** of knowledge. The gift of the **WORD** of knowledge is when the Holy Spirit quickens to your heart information of which you have no natural knowledge. The scriptures declare that we should desire spiritual gifts, in order that we can see people set free.

The Book of Galatians declares that the person who ministers to us, through the Spirit, does it by faith. All the gifts of the Spirit operate by faith in Christ Jesus. One of the major ways that faith comes is by the written **WORD** of God. Faith is when the **WORD** of God becomes more real to you than the natural world you live in. The particular scripture that I decided to meditate on is discovered in 1 Corinthians, chapter 14:

I Corinthians 14:24-25, But if all prophesy, and there come in one that believeth not, or one unlearned, he is convinced of all, he is judged of all: 25 And thus are the secrets of his heart made manifest; and so falling down on his face he will worship God, and report that God is in you of a truth.

I took this scripture and memorized it. Not only did I memorize it, but I meditated on it day and night. I kept speaking it to myself, over and over, very slowly and passionately. I did this until it was burning in my heart. It became more real to me than what was around me. This is a major key to the increasing of faith. It is very similar to the development and the building of physical muscles, and so it is with faith. Immediately, I began to operate in a more precise **WORD** of knowledge.

Here is an illustration. At a midweek service, as I was ministering, a lady walked into the back of our church. She was a first-time visitor, who I had never met before. This particular lady looked to be in her fifties. I was just finishing my message when the Spirit of God quickened my heart to call her forward. When she came to the front of the church, I heard the still small voice of God. I simply repeated what I heard, and out of my mouth came these **WORD**s: "You have one son and two daughters. One daughter is married to a man who is physically abusing her. You are in tremendous fear for her life." I began to speak to her in great detail about what was happening in her life.

What is so amazing, is that when I operate in this realm I remember very little of what I speak. As I continued to prophesy she began to weep and cry, almost uncontrollably, as she literally threw herself to the floor. God brought about an amazing deliverance. She began to proclaim that everything I said was true. And that it was God speaking through me, to her, in a very precise way. I stood there in amazement as I witnessed 1 Corinthians 14 being fulfilled in exactly the way that it proclaimed it would: "And thus are the secrets of his heart made manifest; and so falling down on his face he will worship God, and report that God is in you of a truth."

God is not a respecter of persons; if we give ourselves to the **WORD** of God, and meditate upon it day and night, it will surely come to pass! I could write a book on just this particular way that God speaks. This is one of the major ways that I hear the voice of God in my life, on a daily basis. It is the will of God for every one of His people to hear His still small voice. As you meditate upon these biblical truths, confessing and agreeing with them, the voice of God will become very clear and precise.

Genesis 3:8 And they heard the voice of the LORD God walking in the garden in the cool of the day: and Adam and his wife hid themselves from the presence of the LORD God amongst the trees of the garden.

Her Hair Caught ONFIRE!

I have discovered through the years that when the spirit of God quickens my heart to do something, it is not the time to think, but it is time to act. I cannot tell you how many times I have immediately responded to the spirit of God to a certain situation. As I look back, I realize if I had not quickly done that which the spirit of God quickened to my heart, the end results would have been terrible and devastating. This is one of those situations.

Our youth had been practicing a wonderful Christmas Carol, in which we had a large children's choir. The men of the church had built small risers in which the youth and the children could stand upon. Starting from the front to the back, it took each child up approximately six inches. In one part of the production all the children held lit candles. Almost all the lights were turned off in the sanctuary during this time. It was a beautiful scene, with all the children having their candles lit and singing wonderful Christmas carols to the congregation.

One of our youth was a young attractive teenager who was approximately fourteen years old. Her name was Britney, who had long brown hair. She was standing approximately three rows deep on the third riser. I believe I was sitting on the front row of the chairs in a sanctuary, simply enjoying this wonderful performance of the youth. As I was watching the candlelight, singing performance I noticed something very peculiar. A very light blue haze appeared over the top of Britney's head. Immediately I knew in my heart that her hair was on fire.

One of the teenagers behind her had accidentally put her candle up against Britney's hair. Britney must have used some type of hairspray to be pre-prepared for tonight's performance, and this hairspray was extremely flammable. In my heart I knew that this could be a very devastating situation. I discovered later, that this thought was truly from God. Here is some devastating information about the tragedies resulting from hair fires.

One of the most common characteristics of hair fires is that they are unexpected. Rarely does anyone set his or her hair on fire intentionally. Therefore, when a hair fire happens, the person is caught completely off guard and very often their instinctive reactions make it worse. The most immediate preferred reactions would be to immediately douse the head with water or to smother the fire with a towel, blanket or other suitable material. However, what typically happens is that the person will run about or drop and roll, which only fans the fire with air.

Another reaction to a hair fire is to attempt to put out the fire by the use of hands, which typically results in hand and arm burns. – [Burns typical of a hair fire due to drop down]. Because burning hair will often "drop down," the person receives burns to the neck, shoulders and chest, sometimes to a greater degree than burns to the scalp. The individual's clothing may also catch on fire exacerbating these types of neck, shoulder and chest burns.

Another characteristic of a hair fire is that the person often believes they have successfully extinguished the fire and will stop their efforts to put out the fire only to find that it "re-ignites" In reality, the hair fire does not "re-ignite," but was never completely put out in the first place. If any small portion of the hair remains on fire, it will "re-ignite" the remaining hair. The final characteristic of hair fires is severe disfigurement requiring extensive plastic surgery to correct.

Of course I had no knowledge of any of this at the time, all I had was a quickening, and a super natural urgency entering my heart to get to Britney. I immediately jumped up out of my chair, running for the choir, manoeuvring pass all the other people in the play, and getting past all the props. In my supernatural rush to get to Brittany, not one time did I stumble, trip over a cord, bump into a person, or knock anything over. It is hard for me to explain to people this supernatural realm I enter in when the spirit of God takes me over.

When I finally reached the bleachers, Britney's hair was glowing bluer than ever. Somehow I got in between the children to Brittany. Of course everybody saw all my actions, and had no idea what was happening. To this day many of them that were at this performance never knew what happened.

When I finally stood in front of Britney, in my heart I knew what I needed to do. I could not use my hands to put out her hair fire. Instead, somehow I grabbed the back of her head, (with her hair all burning blue now) pulling her head down to my chest. I took my suit jacket and completely enveloped her head into my chest. Miraculously, yes supernaturally I was able to get her hair extinguished in a matter of seconds.

Britney had no idea what was going on until after the service. Once the fire was out, I did not even say a **WORD** to her or anyone. I just simply helped her stand back up straight, spun around, and went back to my chair. As I think back on this particular situation, I'm sure it looked a little bit comical. The performance never stopped. The play continued, with the choir singing, holding their candle lights. In the minds of the people it was just a little burp in the performance. Thank God for the Holy Ghost, and divine intervention. I believe it was even supernatural that neither one of us received any burns whatsoever.

Meditation upon God's WORD Brings Dreams and Divine Down Loads.

Dreams are mentioned over eighty-seven times in the scriptures. What is a dream? According to Webster's Third New International Dictionary: 1a: a series of thoughts, images, or emotions occurring during sleep ... having ideas or images in the mind while asleep. Therefore, dreams are thoughts and images that occur during sleep. In the scriptures dreams are also called "a vision of the night."

Job 33:15 In a dream, in a vision of the night, when deep sleep falleth upon men, in slumberings upon the bed;

Daniel 4:5 I saw a dream which made me afraid, and the thoughts upon my bed and the visions of my head troubled me.

Daniel 7:1 In the first year of Belshazzar king of Babylon Daniel had a dream and visions of his head upon his bed: then he wrote the dream, and told the sum of the matters.

Daniel 7:7,13 After this I saw in the night visions, ... 13 I saw in the night visions ...

Granted, the above references from the Book of Daniel are in reference to dreams given miraculously by God. However, even when the **WORD** speaks of a "normal" type of dream, it is still called a "night vision" (see Isaiah 29:7-8). In fact, Job 33:15 clearly describes a dream as "a vision of the night." The scriptures also define dreams as "night visions."

God uses dreams to speak to people to a greater extent than we understand or realize. The Book of Job shares a powerful scripture dealing with this subject:

Job 33:14-16 For God speaketh once, yea twice, [yet man] perceiveth it not. 15 In a dream, in a vision of the night, when deep sleep falleth upon men, in slumberings upon the bed; 16 Then he openeth the ears of men, and sealeth their instruction,

According to scientific research, the average person experiences approximately ten dreams every night. Those who have researched this subject say the last twenty minutes before you go to bed determines, to a great extent, what you dream about. On average, most people dream for about two hours every night. Furthermore, we will have over 2,200 dreams in a typical year.

 It is fairly obvious that a lot of dreams people experience are not from the Lord. Yet, you would be amazed by how many of these dreams are coming from God. What you meditate on, watch, and think about - throughout the day - has a powerful impact upon what you will dream about. For instance, if you worry a lot, then you will have dreams pertaining to what you are worrying about. What you do, what you say, and what you meditate upon will be the foremost thoughts in your mind. Your mind is like an incubator: whatever you allow your thought life to become impregnated with, will cause you to give birth - in the area of images and dreams.

Are we responsible for our dreams? Clearly, Job gives an example whereby his dreams tormented him:

Job 7:13-15 When I say, My bed shall comfort me, my couch shall ease my complaint; 14 Then thou scarest me with dreams, and terrifiest me through visions: 15 So that my soul chooseth strangling, [and] death rather than my life.
If our hearts have the power to influence what we dream; then, yes, to some extent we are responsible for what we dream. The dreams we experience will be based upon our lifestyle, our daily meditations, and purpose for living.

Proverbs 23:7 For as he thinketh in his heart, so is he: Eat and drink, saith he to thee; but his heart is not with thee.

We are also responsible for how we respond to situations we find ourselves in – whether we are awake or while we are asleep. If we lust after something, or someone, in our dreams, we are still responsible before God. If we carry out an ungodly act in a dream, we are responsible before God for this act. It is not the devil that causes us to react in a sinful way in a dream. Even if the devil did influence us to do something wrong (awake or asleep) we are still responsible before God for our actions. Amazingly, on the flip side of the coin, we can also be blessed because of our response in a dream. Solomon, the son of David, is a perfect example of this.

1 Kings 3:5-6 In Gibeon the LORD appeared to Solomon in a dream by night: and God said, Ask what I shall give thee. 6 And Solomon said, Thou hast shewed unto thy servant David my father great mercy, according as he walked before thee in truth, and in righteousness, and in uprightness of heart with thee; and thou hast kept for him this great kindness, that thou hast given him a son to sit on his throne, as [it is] this day.

1 Kings 3:10-11 And the speech pleased the Lord, that Solomon had asked this thing. 11 And God said unto him, Because thou hast asked this thing, and hast not asked for thyself long life; neither hast asked riches for thyself, nor hast asked the life of thine enemies; but hast asked for thyself understanding to discern judgment;

There are such things as demonic dreams. Many times, the enemy will attack us in the night, when we seem to be the most vulnerable. Yet, thank the Lord, we are not completely defenseless in these moments if we have a heart after God, and have filled our hearts with the **WORD** of God. Let me share one such experience with you.

We Are Living In Very Dangerous Times

There are many deceivers and false prophets that have entered into the body of Christ. We truly need to be led by the Spirit of God in every decision we make. In all of our associations with people, we have to really become sensitive to what the Spirit of the Lord is saying. I am not talking about having a critical or faultfinding attitude or being paranoid, but being sensitive to the Holy Spirit. Jesus warned us in **John 10:10 The thief cometh not, but for to steal, and to kill, and to destroy.** When the peace and the joy of the Lord is not manifested, we need to stop and ask: "Father, what is going on?"

You might ask: "Pastor Mike, how will I know that God is speaking to me when it comes to peace and joy?" I want to use the **WORD** "feeling" but it is way more than just a feeling or a sensation that comes from your heart. There are times when I see something in my spirit, or I perceive something, or I do not have peace, but I just keep my mouth shut and simply wait upon the

Lord. It might be two weeks, or maybe even three weeks of simply being quiet before the Lord. The scripture that has helped me many times in these situations is:

Proverbs 29:11 A fool uttereth all his mind: but a wise man keepeth it in till afterwards.

Another scripture that I really love, and we all need revelation on is **Ecclesiastes 2:14 The wise man's eyes are in his head; but the fool walketh in darkness: …**

Speaking as a pastor, there are many times people have tried to keep important information from me. They say to themselves: "we really do not want to bother the pastor with this problem or situation" but without them telling me, I know by the Spirit of God what is happening. Sometimes I cannot put my finger on it, but if I simply wait on the Lord for long enough it will manifest, even as the Bible says that everything that is done in secret will be made manifest.

John 14:27 Peace I leave with you, my peace I give unto you: not as the world giveth, give I unto you. Let not your heart be troubled, neither let it be afraid.

I have discovered that many people in the body of Christ are extremely tormented, confused, discouraged and even bitter. Brothers and sisters, this should not be within the body of Christ. Realize that when you are in any of these conditions, you are, to some extent, out of the will of God. There are many different ways in which you can be out of the will of God without even knowing it.

For instance, Job was a righteous man, and yet he was absolutely out of the will of God in his attitude, his **WORD**s, in how he perceived what was happening to him and his family. He sincerely thought it was God that was causing all of the destruction, death, and disaster. He was making such foolish statements; he even stated that it would have been better if he had never been born. He completely lost all his peace and joy. Furthermore, before he was attacked by the devil, he was tormented by fear. Whenever you do not have peace and joy, you need to STOP and ask God what is going on.

1 John 4:18 There is no fear in love; but perfect love casteth out fear: because fear hath torment. He that feareth is not made perfect in love.

Many believers have no peace or joy in their lives. They spend all of their money and time on useless and vain pursuits, trying to find satisfaction and fulfillment. Real peace and joy only comes from Christ, and by being in the middle of His will. When Job finally had a visitation from God, and he saw the error of his ways; repenting, peace, and joy came flooding into his heart and soul; like a mighty River, and Prosperity once again overtook him.

Job 42:5-6, 10 I have heard of thee by the hearing of the ear: but now mine eye seeth thee. 6 Wherefore I abhor myself, and repent in dust and ashes. […] 10 And the LORD turned the captivity of Job, when he prayed for his friends: also the LORD gave Job twice as much as he had before.

According to a new study by Medco Health Solutions (2008), more than one in five Americans were known to take at least one drug to treat a psychological disorder. The drugs range from antidepressants, like Prozac, to anti-anxiety drugs like Xanax. Americans take a startling amount of mental-health related medications. Depression is rampant among the young, and the old. Most cases of alcoholism and drug use are based upon the fact that people are tormented. They are trying to find some way of escaping from their torment.

Proverbs 14:12 There is a way which seemeth right unto a man, but the end thereof are the ways of death.

Drugs, alcohol, materialism, and vain amusements will not bring the ultimate peace and joy that people desire. They will do the Opposite.

THEY WILL DESTROY YOUR WALK WITH GOD!

Psalm 16:11 Thou wilt shew me the path of life: in thy presence is fulness of joy; at thy right hand there are pleasures for evermore.

This is a major KEY: when you lose your peace do not ignore it, but stop and find out why you lost it. I am not suggesting that you lean to the understanding of your mind, but you simply get before the Lord and ask Him what is wrong. You need to start speaking and meditating upon the truths of God's **WORD**, quoting scriptures to yourself dealing with the subject that you need victory in.

I guarantee you, in the midst of this, the Lord will start speaking to you. You should be ready to hear from God by having some paper and a pen in hand. Expect God to speak to you. You should do a quick scan over all your relationships with all of the different people you know, and all of the recent decisions you have made, or are about to make. The Spirit of the Lord will cause you to see what is wrong, and it will almost seem like you are trying to put a square block into a round hole.

CHAPTER EIGHT

Smith Wigglesworth

The **WORD** of God is extremely important, and when we read it, we do so with purpose of heart to obey its every precept. We have no right to open the **WORD** of God carelessly or indifferently. I have no right to come to you with any message unless it is absolutely in agreement with the perfect order of God. I believe we are in Gods will to consider the subject of the Holy Ghost. It is so necessary to be rightly informed about the Spirit in these days when so many people are receiving the Baptism of the Holy Ghost, but are yet so ignorant on this subject

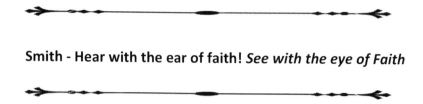

Smith - Hear with the ear of faith! *See with the eye of Faith*

The Way to Overcome is by Believing God's WORD

First John 5. The greatest weakness in the world is unbelief. The greatest power is the faith that works by love. Love, mercy, and grace are bound eternally to faith. There is no fear in love and no question as to being caught up when Jesus comes. The world is filled with fear, torment, remorse, and brokenness, but faith and love are sure to overcome. "Who is he that overcomes the world, but he that believes that Jesus is the Son of God?" (1 John 5:5). God hath established the earth and humanity on the lines of faith. As you come into line, fear is cast out, the **WORD** of God comes into operation and you find bedrock. The way to overcome is to believe Jesus is the Son of God. The commandments are wrapped up in it.

When there is a fidelity between you and God and the love of God is so real that you feel you could do anything for Jesus, all the promises are yea and amen to those who believe. Your life is centered there. Always overcoming what is in the world.

Who keeps the commandments? The born of God. "Ye are of God, little children, and have overcome them: because greater is he that is in you, than he that is in the world" (1 John 4:4). They that believe, love. When did He love us? When we were in the mire. What did He say? Thy sins are forgiven thee. Why did He say it? Because He loved us. What for? That He might bring many sons into glory. His object? That we might be with Him forever. All the pathway is an education for this high vocation and calling. This hidden mystery of love to us, the undeserving!

For our sins the double blessing. "…whatsoever is born of God overcomes the world: and this is the victory…even our faith" (1 John 5:4). He who believes – to believe is to overcome. On the way to Emmaus Jesus, beginning from Moses and all the prophets, interpreted to them in all the Scriptures the things concerning Himself (Luke 24:27). He is the root! In Him is life. When we receive Christ, we receive God and the promises (Galatians 3:29), that we might receive the promise of the Spirit through faith. I am heir to all the promises because I believe. A great heirship! I overcome because I believe the truth. The truth makes me free.

TONGUES AND INTERPRETATION: "It is God who exalts, God who makes rich. The Lord in His mighty arms bears thee up – it is the Lord that encompasses round about thee. When I am weak, then I am strong."

No wavering! This is the principle. He who believes is definite, and because Jesus is in it, it will come to pass. He is the same yesterday, today, and forever (Hebrews 13:8). They that are poor in spirit are heirs to all. There is no limit to the power, for God is rich to all who call upon Him. Not the will of the flesh, but of God (John 1:13). Put in your claim for your children, your families, your co-workers, that many sons may be brought to glory (Hebrews 2:10), for it is all on the principle of faith.

There is nothing in my life or ambition equal to my salvation, a spiritual revelation from heaven according to the power of God, and it does not matter how many flashlights Satan sends through the human mind; roll all on the blood. Who overcomes? He who believes Jesus is the Son (1 John 5:5). God calls in the person with no credentials, it's the order of faith, He who believes overcomes – will be caught up. The Holy Ghost gives revelation all along the line. He that is not against us is for us, and some of the most godly have not touched Pentecost yet.

We must have a good heart especially to the household of faith. "…If any man love the world, the love of the Father is not in him" (1 John 2:15). The root principle of all truth in the human heart is Christ, and when grafted deeply there are a thousand lives you may win. Jesus is the way, the truth, and the life (John 14:6), the secret to every hard problem in the world.

You can't do it! Joseph could not! Everything depends on the principles in your heart. If God dwells in us the principle is light, it comprehends darkness. If thine eye be single, thy whole body shall be full of light, breaking through the hardest thing. "Herein is our love made perfect, that we may have boldness in the day of judgment: because as he is, so are we in this world (1 John 4:17) – for faith has full capacity. When man is pure and it is easy to detect darkness, he that hath this hope purifies himself (1 John 3:3).

TONGUES AND INTERPRETATION: "God confirms in us faith that we may be refined in the world, having neither spot nor blemish nor any such thing. It is all on the line of faith, he that hath faith overcomes – it is the Lord Who purifies and bringeth where the fire burns up all the dross, and anoints with fresh oil; see to it that ye keep pure. God is separating us for Himself.

"…I will give you a mouth and wisdom, which all your adversaries will not be able to gainsay nor resist" (Luke 21:15). The Holy Spirit will tell you in the moment what you shall say. The world will not understand you, and you will find as you go on with God that you do not under-stand fully. We cannot comprehend what we are saved to, or from. None can express the joy of God's indwelling. The Holy Spirit can say through you the need of the moment. The world knows us not because it knew Him not.

"Who is he that overcomes the world, but he that believes Jesus is the Son of God?" (1 John 5:5). A place of confidence in God, a place of prayer, a place of knowledge, that we have what we ask, because we keep His commandments and do the things that are pleasing in His sight. Enoch before his translation had the testimony, he had been well-pleasing unto God. We overcome by believing.

First Published in Flames of Fire p. 2 March 1917

So the **WORD** of God reveals varieties of gifts, meaning that these gifts perfectly meet the condition of people in their individual positions. That is God's plan. Not one person, it may be, would be led out to claim all gifts.

Nevertheless, do not be afraid; the Scriptures are absolute. Paul said that you need not come behind in any gift. God has for you wonderful things beyond what you have ever known or experienced. The Holy Ghost is so full of the prophetic operation of divine power, that it is marvelous what may happen after the Holy Ghost comes upon you.

The BIBLE is the WORD of God

The BIBLE is the **WORD** of God, it has the truths and whatever people may say of them they stand forever established, unmovable. Not one jot or tittle shall fail of all of God's good promises. His **WORD** will come to pass. In heaven it is settled, on earth it must be made manifest that He is the God of everlasting power.

God wants manifest his miracles and for us to see his glory. He wants us all to be filled with the revelation that He can look upon us and delight in us subduing the world, the flesh, and the devil for the glory of God. You need to realize that you are going to miss a great many miracles if you do not begin to trust and obey the leading of the Spirit. But once you begin to act upon the will of God, you will find that God will strengthen your faith and from that day forward it was stopped taking no for that which God has promised. When will you begin?

Came out to hear the WORD of God

Some years ago I was in Ceylon. In one place the folk complained, "Four days is not much to give us." "No," I said, "but it will be a wonderful time." They said to me, "We are not reaching enough people." I said, "Can you have a meeting early in the morning, at eight o'clock?" They said they would. So I said, "Tell all the mothers who want their babies to be healed to come, and all the people over seventy to come, and after that we hope to give an address to the people to get them ready for the Baptism in the Spirit."

It would have done you good to see the four hundred mothers

coming at eight o'clock in the morning with their babies, and then to see the hundred and fifty old people, with their white hair, coming to be healed. We need to have something more than smoke to touch the people; we need to be a burning fire for God. His ministers must be flames of fire. In those days there were thousands out to hear the **WORD** of God. I believe there were about three thousand persons crying for mercy at once in a meeting. It was an amazing and great sight.

From that first morning on the meetings grew to such an extent that I would estimate every time some 5,000 to 6,000 gathered; and I had to preach in a temperature of 110 degrees. Then I had to pray for these people who were sick. But I can tell you, a flame of fire can do anything. Things change in the fire of God.

This was Pentecost. But what moved me more than anything else was this: there were hundreds who tried to touch me, they were so impressed with the power of God that was present. And many testified that with the touch they were healed, it was not that there was any virtue in me—the people's faith was exercised as it was at Jerusalem when they said Peter's shadow would heal them.

You can receive something in three minutes that you can carry with you into glory. **What do you want? Is anything too hard for God?** God can meet you now. God sees inwardly, He knows all about you. Nothing is hidden from Him, and He can satisfy the soul and give you a spring of eternal blessing that will carry you right through.

Jesus is the WORD of God

Why have we power when the Holy Ghost comes? Because the Holy Ghost reveals Jesus; and Jesus is the **WORD** of God. In that **WORD** there is all power. In order to understand what it means to have all power there are two things necessary; **#1** is to have ears to hear and **#2** is to have hearts to receive it.

I am sure that everyone should know this truth that God sent the devil out of heaven because he was evil; if he had been holy he would not have sent him out. You never find anything that is impure get purer, but always viler, and Satan when he was cast out became weaker, viler, and more impure. Every born saint of God, filled with the Spirit, has a real revelation of that truth, **"Greater is he that is in you, than he that is in the world."** [1Jn 4.4] I say this with as much audacity as I can.

I know evil spirits are in abundance and in multitudes beyond count; Jesus cast them out as a legion. Satan and his angels were cast out of heaven and it seems to me that Satan had power to make evil spirits, but these are never as strong as Satan himself.

Because of purity, holiness and righteousness, they that are strong shall become more and more righteous, and equally so. Satan and his emissaries become viler and viler, but also weaker and weaker. But the believer because of the Spirit that is in him has the **power to cast out these evil spirits**. It must be so; God wants us to have this power operating in us; **we must be able to destroy Satan's power wherever we go.**

Thy WORD is Power

The **WORD** of God is wonderful and I believe that God wants to fill us with his **WORD**. He wants us to be so filled with it that no matter where we are, the **WORD** will be lived out in us. The **WORD** is power, the **WORD** is life, the **WORD** of God is faith, the **WORD** is Jesus and the **WORD** of God is everlasting life to him that believeth.

"He that [hath] my WORD, and believeth on him that sent me, hath everlasting life." [Jn 5.24]

We need to be careful in reading the **WORD**; I believe it is too precious to rush over; we have need to **"rightly [divide] the**

WORD of truth." [2Ti 2.15] I want to speak to you about the power given by God. Oh the power of the Holy Ghost! The power that quickens, the revealing power, the travailing power! The power that lives and moves! The power that brings about exactly what Jesus said, **"When you receive... ye shall have power." [Ac 1.8, para.]**

I love to think that Jesus wants all his people to be full of His power, and that he wants all men to be overcomers. It is the joy God brings within a human life that transforms it by his **WORD** and brings us into the place where we know it is above all opposition, and brings to naught the things that are, because God is in the **WORD**. Nothing but Gods power will do it.

Power over sin, power over sickness, power over the devil, power over all the powers of the devil! I know that Jesus revealed by his **WORD** these truths—**"after that ye shall have power." [Ac 1.8, para.]** I think there is nothing more beautiful to experience are own personal Jordan River baptism.

The moment that Jesus was baptized in the Holy Ghost there was a manifestation that never appeared in the world before or since. Right there by the River Jordan was the Son of God baptized in the Holy Ghost. He came upon Jesus in the form of a dove. At that moment in the heavens above came the voice of God. [Lk 3.22] It is beautiful to think of how the Trinity is reaching out to humanity.

"You devil, come out of this man in the name of Jesus."

One day as I was waiting for a car I stepped into a shoemaker's shop. I had not been there long when I saw a man with a green shade over his eyes, crying pitifully and in great agony. It was heartrending and the shoemaker told me that the inflammation was destroying his eyes. I jumped up and went to the man and said, **"You devil, come out of this man in the name of Jesus."**

Instantly the man said, "It is all gone, I can see now." That is the only scriptural way, to begin to work at once, and preach afterwards. You will find as the days go by that miracles and healings will be manifested as act upon the quickening of Gods Spirit! Because the Master was touched with the feeling of the infirmities of the multitudes they instantly gathered around him to hear what He had to say concerning the **WORD** of God.

However, I would rather see one man saved than ten thousand people healed. If you ask me why, I would call to your attention the **WORD** which says, **"There was a [rich man and he] fared sumptuously every day."** [Lk 16.19] Now we don't hear of this man having any diseases but it says, **"In hell he lift up his eyes."** [Lk 16.23] We also read that there was a poor man full of sores [Lk 16.20] and **"he lifted up his eyes in heaven,"** so we see that a man can die practically in good health but be lost, and a man can die in disease and be saved; so it is more important to be saved than anything else.

ZOE

But Jesus was sent to bear the infirmities and the afflictions of the people and to destroy the works of the devil. He said that the thief (which is the devil) **cometh to steal and to kill and to destroy, but "I am come that [ye] might have life, and have it more abundantly."** [Jn 10.10]

I maintain that God wishes all his people to have this (ZOE) life more abundant; that if we understood sin as we ought to understand it and realized that there is no sickness without disobedience, ignorance of Gods will, or lack of Faith! You will say that this is rather strong, but we have the remedy in the**WORD of God**! Jesus paid the full price and the full redemption for every need, and where sin abounded, grace can come in and much more abound, [Ro 5.20] and dispel all the sickness.

God moved me on to a place of increasing faith, causing me to see that the WORD of God was written to show us how to act on the principles of faith.

The mind of God

What you need is to know the mind of God and the **WORD** of God, and you will be so free you will never find a frown on your face, nor a tear in your eye of unbelief again. The more you know of the mightiness of the revelation of God, the more everything in the way of fearfulness pass away.

To know God, is to be in the place of triumph. To know God is to be in the place of rest. To know God is to be in the place of absolute victory.

The backslider

When we came into this new work God spoke to us by the Spirit and we knew we had to reach the place of absolute submission and cleansing, so that there would be nothing left. We were swept and garnished. Now, that was only the beginning, and if you have not made spiritual progress into that holy place of zeal, power and compassion for God, we can truly say you have backslidden in heart. The backslider in heart is dead to Gods fullness. He is not having the open vision. The backslider in heart is not seeing the **WORD** of God living and fresh every day.

You can put it down that a man is a backslider in heart if does not hate the sinful things of the world. And if you have the applause of the world you do not having the approval of God. I do not know whether you will receive it or not but my heart burns with this message, "changing in the regeneration" for in this changing you will get a place in the kingdom to come where you shall be in authority; that place which God has prepared for us, that place which is beyond all human conception.

We can catch a glimpse of that glory, when we see how John worshipped the angel, and the angel said to him, **"See thou do it not, for I am thy fellow-servant, of thy brethren the prophets."** This angel is showing John the wonders of the glorious kingdom and in his glorified state, John thought he was the Lord. I wonder if we dare believe for this glorious place.

Smith : "You must be yielded to the WORD of God. The WORD will cause love to begin to flow in our hearts like a River, and when divine love is in our hearts, there is no room to boast about ourselves. We see ourselves as nothing when we get lost in this divine love."

I want to impress upon you the importance of believing what the SCRIPTURE says, and I have many things to relate about people who dared to believe God and his **WORD** until it came to pass.

This is a wonderful reality. In fact, all of the **WORD** of God is a wonderful reality. It is an everlasting **WORD**, a **WORD** of power, a **WORD** of health, a **WORD** of substance, a **WORD** of life. It produces life into the very nature, to everyone that lays hold of it, if he believes. I want you to understand that there is a need for the **WORD** of God that brings us the blessing.

"He that looketh shall be healed."

Now listen! Some people put the touch of the Lord in the place of faith. The Lord would not have that woman believe that the touch had done it. She felt as soon as she touched him that virtue had gone through her, [Mk 5.29] which is true. When the people were bitten by fiery serpents in the wilderness, God's **WORD** said through Moses, **"He that looketh shall be healed."** [Nu 21.8] The look made it possible for God to do it. Did the touch heal the woman?

Transformed by Eating Royal Jelly

No, the touch meant something more, it was an act of living faith. Jesus said, **"Thy faith hath made thee whole." [Mk 5.34]** Her Faith in Jesus. If God would just move on us to believe, there would not be a sick person who could not receive healing.

As soon as this woman in the street, with all the crowd about her, began to testify, the devil came. The devil is always in a testimony meeting. When the sons of God gathered together in the time of Job, he was there. **[Jb 1.6]**

While this was happening in the street, three persons came rushing from the house of Jairus and said, "There is no use now, your daughter is dead. They thought Jesus can do nothing for a dead daughter. Your wife needs you at home." But Jesus said, **"Be not afraid, only believe." [Mk 5.35-36]** He speaks the **WORD** just in time! Jesus is never to late. When the trouble is the worst, the pain the most severe, the cancer gripping the body, then the **WORD** comes, **"Only believe."** When everything seems as though it will fail, and is practically hopeless, the **WORD** of God comes to us, **"Only believe."**

When Jesus came to that house there were a lot of people weeping and wailing. [Mk 5.38] I have taken my last wreath to the cemetery. To be absent from the body is to be present with the Lord, [2Co 5.8] and if you believe that, you will never take another wreath to the cemetery. It is unbelief that mourns. If you have faith that they are with the Lord you will never take another flower to the grave. They are not there. Hallelujah!

These people were standing around, weeping, wailing and howling. He says, **"Why make you this to-do? The maid is not dead, but sleepeth." [Mk 5.39]** There is a wonderful **WORD** that God wants you to hear. Jesus said, **"I am the resurrection and the life." [Jn 11.25]** The believer may fall asleep, but the believer doesn't die. Oh, that people would understand the deep things of God, it would change the whole situation. It makes you look out with a glorious hope to the day when the Lord shall come. What does it say? **"They that sleep will God bring with him." [1Th 4.14]** Jesus knew that.

"The maid is not dead, but sleepeth; and they laughed him to scorn." [Mt 9.24] To show the insincerity of these wailers, they could turn from wailing to laughing. Jesus took the father and the mother of the maid and going into the room where she was took her hand and said, **"Daughter, arise." And the child sat up. [Mk 5.40-42]** Praise the Lord! And he said, **"Give her something to eat." [Mk 5.43]**

"Be not afraid, only believe."

Oh, the remarkableness of our Lord Jesus! I want to impress upon you the importance of realizing that Jesus is in the midst. No person need be without the knowledge that they are not only saved, but that God can live in their bodies.

You are begotten the moment you believe, unto a lively hope. **"He that believeth hath eternal life." [Jn 3.36]** You have eternal life the moment you believe. The first life is temporal, natural, material, but in the new birth you exist as long as God Himself! Forever! And we are begotten by an incorruptible power, by the **WORD** of God. The new birth is unto righteousness, begotten by God the moment that you believe. God always saves through the heart. **He that believeth in his heart and confesseth with his mouth shall be saved. [Ro 10.9]**

Jesus is here tonight to lose them that are bound. If you are suffering in your body, he will heal you now as we pray. He is saying to every sin-sick soul, to every disease-smitten one, **"Be not afraid, only believe."** Be wide awake.

Holy Thoughtfulness

Let us enter into these great **WORD**s on the line of holy thoughtfulness. If I go on with God He wants me to understand all His deep things. He doesn't want anybody in the Pentecostal church to be novices, or to deal with the **WORD** of God on natural grounds. We can understand the **WORD** of God only by the Spirit of God.

We cannot define, or separate, or deeply investigate and unfold this holy plan of God without we have the life of God, the thought of

God, the Spirit of God, and the revelation of God. The **WORD** of Truth is pure, spiritual, and divine. If you try to divide it on natural grounds you will only finish up on natural lines for natural man, but you will never satisfy a Pentecostal Assembly.

The people who are spiritual can only be fed on spiritual material. So if you are expecting your messages to catch fire you will have to have them on fire. You won't have to light the message up in the meeting. You will have to bring the message red-hot, burning, living.

The message must be direct from heaven. It must be as truly, "Thus saith the Lord," as the Scriptures which are, "Thus saith the Lord," because you will only speak as the Spirit gives utterance, and you will always be giving fresh revelation. You will never be stale on any line, whatever you say will be fruitful, elevating the mind, lifting the people, and all the people will want more.

The Plumb Line

The BIBLE is the plumb line of everything. And without we are plumbed right up with the **WORD** of God, we will fail in the measure in which we are not righteous. And so may God the Holy Ghost bring us, this morning, into that blessed ministry of righteousness. Amen! Glory to God!

The Perfect Mirror

As we look into the perfect mirror of the face of the Lord we are changed from one state of grace to another, from glory to glory. You will never find anything else but the **WORD** of God that takes you there. So you cannot afford to put aside that **WORD**.

I beseech you, beloved, that you come short of none of these beatitudes w have been speaking of, in your life. These grand truths of the **WORD** of God must be your testimony, must be your life, your pattern. You must be in it, in fact you are of it. "Ye are...the epistle of Christ," God says to you by the Spirit. Then let us see that we put off everything that by the grace of God we may put on everything.

Where there is a standard which hasn't been reached in your life, God in His grace, by His mercy and your yieldedness, can fit you for that place that you can never be prepared for only by a broken heart and a contrite spirit, yielding to the will of God. If you will come with a whole heart to the throne of grace, God will meet you and build you on His spiritual plane. Amen. Praise the Lord!

We have a big God. We have a wonderful Jesus. We have a glorious Comforter. God's canopy is over you and will cover you at all times, preserving you from evil. Under His wings shalt thou trust. The **WORD** of God is living and powerful and in its treasures you will find eternal life. If you dare trust this wonderful Lord, this Lord of life, you will find in Him everything you need.

CHAPTER NINE

HOW GOD TOOK ME DEEP INTO HIS WORD

They Took Four Offerings in One Service

My family and I were ready for vacation. We wanted to go somewhere and get refreshed spiritually. Because of the fact that we do not watch TV, we really did not know about the different ministries. We were encouraged to go to a well-known minister in Ohio who had a camp meeting every year. Supposedly, they had wonderful and amazing meetings. We bundled up the children and packed everything for one week of vacation.

We were on our way for an exciting and spiritual vacation, or so we thought. We arrived in Ohio just before the camp meeting was to start. We entered the parking lot of this large and impressive church, which had acres of parking. The worship and praise was wonderful and exciting with lots of enthusiasm. But pretty soon our joy was brought down a couple of notches. What caused this unexpected disappointment was how they aggressively went after raising money.

I never have been one for all of this hype and high-pressure tactics for money. It is not because we're not givers; many times we have given up to ninety percent of our income on a regular basis. To be honest with you, I've known some of the top money raisers in the religious world. One of the best-known money raisers years ago was ministering in our church.

When he began to make wild promises to our congregation about how wealthy they would become if they would just give a certain amount of money, I basically had to put a stop to it. I took him out to eat and I tried to talk some godly wisdom into him. For over two hours I began to show him with the Scriptures that he was getting the people to be involved in idolatry and spiritual gambling. I showed him that he was taking advantage of people in their desperation, and this was absolutely against the teachings of Christ.

I thought he had received what I said, because of the conviction that was evident upon him. So, a year later when he was coming through our area wanting to speak at our church again, I decided to give him another opportunity; which was a big mistake. Praise God we had a heavy snowfall during the week he was to be with us, and very few people came to this meeting. I'm sorry to say that he was worse now than ever. He even was extremely upset because our turnout was so small.

Back to Our Ohio Vacation:

After the first night of meetings in Ohio, we went back to our hotel extremely disappointed. The next morning I said to the Lord, "Father, help me to keep my heart right with You. I do not want to be judgmental of these people." Once again, right after the worship, tremendous pressure was applied to the people to give in order to get back something from God. I sat there deciding to grin and bear it. After this fund-raising endeavor, there were some other announcements and activities with special singing and testimonies.

Then once again, they started raising money.

This time I said, "Lord, if they raise money one more time, we are walking out of here and going home." A well-known speaker got up ministering a powerful message on how to win your whole household to the Lord. Now this was exciting what he was preaching, I could really get into this. He was ministering out of the book of Acts chapter 16 verse 31. But to my extreme disappointment, when he declared that if you wanted this scripture to work for you, then you were going to have to sow a seed of $16.31 for every person you wanted to be saved. Surely people had enough spirituality not to fall for this trickery. Yet that was not the case, people fell for it.

I could no longer take this manipulation and trickery. We got up, left, and I packed up my wife and children to go home. We checked out of the hotel and drove all the way back home to Pennsylvania. As I was driving home, in my heart I was complaining about these people.
Then the Spirit of the Lord spoke to me, not agreeing or disagreeing pertaining to these people.

Favorite Scripture Preacher

The Lord started to bring discipline into my life about my spiritual condition. He basically told me that I was a "favorite scripture" preacher, and that I really did not know His Word the way that I should. I was so convicted by this confrontation from God, that I made a commitment: I would begin to pour myself into the Bible, like never before. I was going to spend hours in God's Word and in prayer.

When I arrived home from my vacation, I informed my staff that I was going to give myself to long hours of prayer and the Word. I began with the Book of Ephesians; starting with the very first chapter. I did not only want to memorize it, I wanted to get it into my heart. This took me close to three weeks, and countless hours to memorize.

The next mountain I climbed was the Book of Galatians. As I was memorizing the scriptures and chapters of the Bible, I was getting terrible headaches. But I kept working at it because I knew that without pain, there is no gain. When I had conquered Galatians, I moved to the Book of Philippians.

Brain Quickening Experience

One day, as I was into the second chapter of Philippians; something supernatural and amazing took place. I had what the Bible calls an "open vision." This happens when you are wide awake, and yet everything disappears around you - except what God is showing you.

In the open vision, right in front of me appeared a very large body of water. It was pure blue, with not one ripple upon it. It stretched as far as the natural eye could see, in every direction. The room I was in had completely gone - there was nothing but this gigantic blue lake. As I lifted my head to look into the light-blue, never-ending, and cloudless sky; I saw a large, crystal-clear raindrop falling down from the heavens, in slow-motion, heading towards the body of water. I watched in amazement as it slowly came tumbling down towards this lake. When it hit the surface of the body of water, it caused ripples to flow forth.

As the ripples flowed forth from the center of where the drop had hit, they began to grow in size and intensity. Then, as suddenly as the vision had come, it was gone. I stood in my office in complete amazement; not understanding what had just happened, or, indeed, why it had happened.

I knew that this experience was from God, but I did not know what the significance of it was. I knew in my heart that God eventually would show me what it meant. When the Lord gives me a supernatural visitation, I do not try to understand with my natural mind. I simply give it to the Lord knowing that in His time, He will show me what the experience means or what He was saying.

I picked up my Bible and went back to memorizing scriptures. I immediately noticed there was a change in my mental capacity. It seemed as if my brain was absorbing the Word of God like a dry sponge soaking up water. Within one-hour, I memorized a whole chapter of the Book of Philippians - as if it were nothing.

I was amazed! Before this, it took me days to memorize a chapter and yet, now I could memorize a chapter in an hour. I continued to memorize books of the Bible until there were nine books inside of me. This is not including thousands of other scriptures that I continued to memorize while dealing with certain subjects.

I honestly believe that I could have memorized the whole New Testament, had I not allowed the activities of ministry to overwhelm me, and keep me preoccupied. The enemy of our soul knows how to make things happen in our lives to get us sidetracked.

Why in the world would God open up my heart and mind in such a dramatic way to memorize the Word? Because it is by the Word of God that our minds are renewed, and we can discover His perfect will for our lives. The Word of God has the capacity to quicken our minds and mortal bodies.

God's Word is awesome, quick, and powerful. I believe there is an activation of the things of the Spirit when we begin to give ourselves one-hundred-percent to whatever it is God has called us to do. There is a dynamic principle of laying your life down in order to release the aroma of heaven.

2 Corinthians 12:2-4 I knew a man in Christ above fourteen years ago, (whether in the body, I cannot tell; or whether out of the body, I cannot tell: God knoweth;) such an one caught up to the third heaven. 3 And I knew such a man, (whether in the body, or out of the body, I cannot tell: God knoweth;) 4 How that he was caught up into paradise, and heard unspeakable words, which it is not lawful for a man to utter.

I'm sorry to say, though, that I became so busy running the church, Christian school, a small bible college, radio station, TV broadcasting and construction projects, twenty-five churches in the Philippines, not including other aspects of being a pastor, that I did not continue in memorizing the Bible.

Through the years though, I've had an insatiable hunger for the Word of God. God has allowed me to write over seven thousand sermons, 30 books, and to do many things that I never have been taught or trained to do. In the midst of all these activities I have earned a PhD in biblical theology and I received a Doctorate of Divinity. I believe it is all because of the divine supernatural visitations and quickening's of God's Holy Spirit. The reason why I believe we do not experience more of these visitations is because of a lack of spiritual hunger. If we would hunger and thirst, God would satisfy these desires.

"Blessed are they which do hunger and thirst after righteousness: for they shall be filled" (Matt 5:6).

"Delight thyself also in the LORD; and he shall give thee the desires of thine heart. Commit thy way unto the LORD; trust also in him; and he shall bring it to pass. And he shall bring forth thy righteousness as the light, and thy judgment as the noonday" (Ps. 37:4-6).

Danny alive on to God

Back in the spring of 2011 my second son, Daniel came to me wanting spiritual direction. He told me that he really wanted to grow spiritually, and wanted my advice on the best way to go about it. I told him if he really wanted to grow spiritually and fast, he would have to give himself to the memorization, and the meditation of God's word.

That he would need to saturate himself with nothing but the Bible. He would need to not just memorize Scriptures, but think them, speak them, sing them, eat them and drink them. That as he would meditate upon God's word, the fires of heaven would to begin to burn in his inner man.

Psalm 39:3 My heart was hot within me, while I was musing the fire burned: then spake I with my tongue,

I told him that all of my amazing experiences, victories, healings, deliverances could be traced back to the word of God which I had hidden in my heart. That it is only the Word of God, quickening our hearts, and renewing our minds which opens the door for God to begin to move in us in a truly powerful and amazing way. I have told many people this through the last over 40 years. Many of these people have read hundreds of my stories, and been extremely blessed, and amazed. I am sorry to say though that the majority of them never have taken to heart my simple instructions.

When I told my son Daniel this truth (which I have taught all of my children) I could see a determination in his eyes to do this exact thing. From that moment forward Daniel began to spend hours every day in nothing but God's word. He cut off any knowledge or information, entertainment, or distracting amusements that would take him away from God's word.

Immediately we began to see a wonderful transformation in his life. His attitude, disposition, even his response to circumstances and situations changed.

Within three months you would not have recognized Daniel from who he was before. Do not get me wrong, he was never a typical pastors son. He had never gone into the drugs, alcohol, rebellion or sexual immorality of the world. I have strived with all the sincerity of my heart to raise my children by example, and by encouragement of what it really means to love God, and to live a godly life. I have been greatly blessed by my three sons, and daughter.

Now it was not just that Danny was living morally upright, but that there was a new fire, a new passion, a new hunger and desire in him to know God. God's word had literally begun to transform him in a wonderful and amazing way. His preaching, and is histestifying became powerful and dynamic. I watched as ***Joshua 1:8*** began to be fulfilled in his life. What God did for my son Daniel he will do for anyone who sincerely hides the word of God in their heart, and lives accordingly.

Joshua 1:8 This book of the law shall not depart out of thy mouth; but thou shalt meditate therein day and night, that thou mayest observe to do according to all that is written therein: for then thou shalt make thy way prosperous, and then thou shalt have good success.

God Moves upon Rapist & Murderers

My 2nd son Daniel and I went to minister in a little country called Suriname (this little nation's population is basically of African slavery descent). While we were there we were invited to a men's high-security prison. They wanted us to speak to young men who had been incarcerated for the serious crimes of murder, rape, and terrible deeds. We agreed to do this. There was a godly young mother who had a burden for these young boys. They were prisoners from 12 years old up to 18. She told us that she had not seen a hardly results even though she had been pouring her life and much prayer into this endeavor. This particular day her prayers finally paid off.

My son Daniel was to be the one to minister to them because he was in his 20s. This precious lady felt that if they heard a young man speak, it might touch them. As my son spoke, he was sharing about his life, but it did not seem like it was having much of, if any effect upon them whatsoever. He finally turned the service over to me.

I began to share my life experience, and how God had delivered me from drugs, alcohol, violence, and running with a gang outside of Chicago. As I was speaking, I happen to look over at my son Daniel, and I saw and perceived that the spirit of God was moving upon him in a mighty way. The hair on the back of my neck literally stood up, the spirit of the Lord was upon him so powerfully. Intermediately I turned this meeting back over to him.

A tremendous prophetic word began to come forth out of his mouth. I can tell you without a shadow of a doubt it was not my son speaking, but the spirit of the living God. He began to talk about a young man named Joseph, and how Joseph had ended up in prison wrongfully. But that he had maintained a spirit of integrity and love for God. That even in prison he never became bitter or angry at God or others. He just kept pressing in and taking a hold of the Lord no matter what his condition or situation was.

Because of Joseph's godly disposition and seeking the Lord that eventually Joseph was put second in charge over all of the land of Egypt (which was the most powerful nation on the world at the time) literally overnight. He told them that no matter why they were there, or their present condition, that if they would truly cry out to

God with all of their hearts, turning their lives over to Jesus they could become a Joseph.

As my son preached underneath this heavy anointing, the spirit of God fell upon these young men. I sat there in utter amazement as I watched an amazing transformation before my eyes as they surrendered their lives to Christ on the spot! When my son was done, the spirit of the Lord had me to have all of them shout in English: I am a Joseph! (English is their primary language) They shouted this phrase over and over.

I will never forget this amazing meeting where the Spirit of God was so tangible that you could cut it with a knife. Now they could not pronounce Joseph the way we do, so they ended up shouting: I Am a YOSEPH! Over and over they shouted: I Am a YOSEPH! The whole prison shook as these approximately 40 young men declaring with all of their hearts and vocal abilities by the spirit of the Lord: I Am a YOSEPH! I Am a YOSEPH! I Am a YOSEPH!

I will never forget that day as long as I live! Both my son and I began to weep for these young men as the spirit of God overwhelmed them. Then my son Daniel and I took every one of those young men one at a time into our arms weeping and praying for them that they would become a Joseph even as they had boldly proclaimed. We all stood there in amazement, and tears as GOD had stepped down from heaven to be with us at that moment!

Weeping, wailing in Surinam

I was ministering in a little country called Suriname, which is located right below Brazil across the Amazon River. A precious brother and pastor from the Baltimore Christian center had arranged for me to be speaking in small gatherings. In these meetings a precious apostolic sister by the name of Rinia Refos, heard me speak. The Lord touched her in such a wonderful way that she wanted me to meet her apostle, who is over one of the largest churches in this nation. She took me to this precious Elderly Apostle. I gave her one of my books about my experience of going to hell. And shared with her some of my testimony.

After we had left this meeting, I think approximately a day later sister Rinia Refos informed me that her apostle would love to have me speak at the next Sunday morning service. I agreed to this request. It came into my heart to begin to prepare for this particular service. I informed my son Daniel and the peoples whose house where I was staying that I would not be eating for a number of days, in order to get the mind of Christ.

It came into my heart that I was to share from memory the book of James. God has allowed me to memorize 10 books of the New Testament including many Scriptures. All I did for approximately 3 days was quote the book of James over and over to myself slowly, meditating upon its wonderful truths.

Back in 1997 when I had originally memorized this book I had informed my congregation that I would be sharing it on a Sunday night. That I would be preaching the book of James from beginning to end by memory. I still remember that amazing night. There were literally hundreds of people who had showed up to watch me proclaim this message. As I was ministering, I could sense a mighty move of God beginning to take place. When I gave the altar call well over 100 people (believers) came running for the altar weeping and wailing. God did a wonderful work that night!

Here I was once again meditating, praying and pondering, musing upon the book of James. The Sunday morning I was to speak finally came. As I entered into the sanctuary, which I believe sits about 3000, it was almost filled to capacity. Now in the natural I'm a little bit nearsighted. This building was narrow and very deep. The stage was about 3 to 4 feet high. The very 1st row of chairs I think was probably about 30 feet away. When I stood upon the stage I could see the 1st couple rolls of people, but from there back it was very blurry.

Now to say that I was pumped up, would not be sufficient to declare how I felt at this moment. I had been fasting and quoting the book of James for 3 days from morning to night. My heart had been filled with the fire of heaven. The lady who was to interpret for me stood by the pulpit. Now this is where I really messed up. I was so pumped up that I was standing on the very edge of the stage as if I was trying to get out to the people.

I am sure they were expecting me to stand right there next to the pulpit. The precious lady who was to interpret for me was behind my back. I had a microphone in my hand, waiting to be released upon these precious people with the truths of the book of James burning in my heart. I have a terrible habit of speaking fast as it is, but now I had to have it interpreted into their language. As I began to speak, rapidly this precious lady kept trying to get me to slow down.

It also seemed to me that the apostle sitting on the front row of chairs, was not very happy with what was going on. In my heart I began to get frustrated with myself, because I felt like I was really messing up. As I continued to preach the book of James from my heart, it seem like things were going from bad to worse. The interpreter kept trying to get me to slow up, turn around and speak to where she could see my lips. I knew that my time was running out, and I really wanted to get to chapter 3 and chapter 4. As I was speaking I saw that there was a lot of motion taking place in the congregation. It seemed to me that people were not wanting to stay in their chairs. I could not really see very well because of my nearsightedness.

I finally came to the place where I knew I had run out of time. I finished up speaking a little bit out of chapter 3 and chapter 4. I felt as if in my heart that if I did not stop soon, they would drag me off of the stage. So in my heart, with utter defeat, I gave the altar call.

Transformed by Eating Royal Jelly

During this whole time there had been movement going on in the congregation. I thought within my mind that they were leaving out of frustration of me speaking so fast, and the interpreter not being able to interpret what I was saying. What a disaster!

When I gave the altar call, something amazing happened. People were running for the front. In a very brief time the whole front of this large sanctuary was filled with people who were weeping and crying. I began to look for workers, altar workers to help with all of these precious people who had come forward. But there was nobody to help. I went down into the mist of them trying to pray for as many as I could. This went on for quite a while. Eventually people began to wander away. In my heart I was so grateful that these people responded to my terrible message, but I still felt like I was a complete failure.

A number of days went by, as I was ministering in other smaller fellowships. The precious sister who had set up these meetings (Rinia Refos) while we were in the car brought up this particular meeting. She said to me: was it not just amazing how God moved in the meeting on Sunday? I was completely baffled by this statement. I asked her to explain what she meant? I told her because of my nearsightedness I could not really tell what was going on.

She told me that as I began to preach and teach from the book of James that literally the power of God had hit the congregation. That as I was preaching people were falling out of their chairs, and being tossed about by the power of God. I could not hardly believe what I was hearing. I knew I had seen movement, but I did not know that it was the Holy Ghost moving. And then she said something that was even more amazing! She told me that it was wonderful when you gave the altar call, and all of those people who had come forward. I told her I was blessed with that also, but I asked her where the leaders were.

That's when she informed me that the most amazing thing about the whole meeting was that all of those people who had come running forward weeping and wailing before God, were the leaders of the church. Yes it was the leaders of the church that God had convicted! For judgment must 1st begin in the house of the Lord. This is the reason why there was nobody there to help pray for them. In spite of my over zealousness, and lack of wisdom God had once again showed up to do a mighty work!

CHAPTER TEN

Amazing Outpourings of the Spirit!

From 1975 up to now there have been times when I have seen God pour out his Spirit upon whole congregations when everybody in the meeting fell out of their chairs, weeping, wailing, and crying. In one meeting everyone melted to the floor under a mighty move of God, with no one moving or speaking for over two hours!

At times people falling under the power of God, and getting up completely healed without anybody laying hands on them. Supernatural manifestations of the Holy Ghost, of God's amazing presence where the wind was blowing in the sanctuaries where there was no Windows, fans, or doors open. A cloud of glory manifested so that you could barely see the person in front of you.

The fragrances of heaven filled the services to where people were trying to discover where the fragrance was coming from. Where at times it felt like it was raining on us physically, but it was the invisible outpouring of the spirit. Where demons would just begin to manifest in people, and we cast them out of the people with just a whisper in the name of Jesus. We're broken bones were instantly healed, tumors banished, hernias instantly gone, and where people could hear angelic beings singing in the services.

These movements of God did not happen as a result of everybody praying or worshiping, fasting or giving financially. It happened because there was at least one person, if not more who were hungering and thirsting after God, believing and trusting Jesus more than anything else. I'm not talking about super spirituality or maturity, but I'm talking about a person or people who simply took a hold of God, and would not let go. What I have seen God do in the last 40 years he will do for anybody who is hungry for him.

Now you might say: Pastor Mike if God has done this for you in the past, then why isn't he doing it in every service you're in? Good question! **It is because many times I'm not consistent in my spiritual pursuit of holiness, obedience, loving God, and giving him my whole heart with utter passion.** The good news though is that it is still available for anyone who wants it! There is a Scripture in second Chronicles that says: the eyes of the Lord run to and fro, throughout the whole earth, to show himself strong, on the behalf of them, whose hearts are perfect towards him. Let us believe God to press in deeper, further, than we have ever gone before.

A perfect heart is one that: #1 loves God, #2 trust God, #3 obeys God, #4 agrees with God, #5 and pursues God with all of their heart. #6 Forsakes Sin! #7 Loves Righteousness & Holiness!

God's Word with Power

I cannot overemphasize the importance of being filled with the Holy Ghost in the declaration and the proclamation of the gospel. Jesus declared that without him we could do nothing. He also declared that it was expedient for him to leave so that the promise of the father would come.

John 16:7 Nevertheless I tell you the truth; It is expedient for you that I go away: for if I go not away, the Comforter will not come unto you; but if I depart, I will send him unto you.

Christ commanded his disciples that they needed to stay in Jerusalem on to the promise of the Father had come. He told them that they would be endued with power from on high. It is after this endowment of the Holy Ghost that there was a dramatic change in the results of their preaching ministry.

Acts 1:4 And, being assembled together with them, commanded them that they should not depart from Jerusalem, but wait for the promise of the Father, which, saith he, ye have heard of me.5 For John truly baptized with water; but ye shall be baptized with the Holy Ghost not many days hence.....8 But ye shall receive power, after that the Holy Ghost is come upon you: and ye shall be witnesses unto me both in Jerusalem, and in all Judaea, and in Samaria, and unto the uttermost part of the earth.

In the Book of Acts is revealed to us a mighty move bringing amazing conviction upon the hearers as Peter proclaimed the gospel.

Acts 2:14 But Peter, standing up with the eleven, lifted up his voice, and said unto them, Ye men of Judaea, and all ye that dwell at Jerusalem, be this known unto you, and hearken to my words:...........SERMON.............36 Therefore let all the house of Israel know assuredly, that God hath made the same Jesus, whom ye have crucified, both Lord and Christ. **37 Now when they heard this, they were pricked in their heart, and said unto Peter and to the rest of the apostles, Men and brethren, what shall we do?**

Amazing conviction fell upon over 3000 men as they heard Peter preach. They all cried out as one: **Men and brethren, what shall we do?** Now you might ask: **How Can This Be Possible?** How could 3000 men ask such a question at the same time? I have personally experienced such movements in my life where everybody who was in the meeting moved in complete harmony under the convicting power of the Holy Ghost.

The Importance of Divine Conviction

So much of the preaching today in the majority of the pulpits not just in America but around the world lacks any power of conviction. When conviction does come to many of those who confess to know Christ, it is rejected as nothing but condemnation. The church is in such a sad condition that it is beyond my ability to express with human words.

There are many examples in the Bible of conviction coming upon the multitudes as the prophets of God declared: **Thus Saith the Lord!** It is this preaching that brought about National Repentance. These profits did not speak of their accord, but under the influence of the Holy Ghost.

2 Peter 1:21 For the prophecy came not in old time by the will of man: but holy men of God spake as they were moved by the Holy Ghost.

Historically we could discover that many of the great revivals and awakenings that have happened through the ages were because there was a Minister, who preached under the divine influence and Power of the Holy Ghost. In this book, we will take a brief look at some of these amazing experiences that these men and women had when the power of God manifested itself in their preaching. We are speaking about such people as, John Wesley, George Whitfield, Jonathan Edwards, Charles Finney, Smith Wigglesworth, Mary Woodworth-Etter,............... Etc.

Transformed by Eating Royal Jelly

There is one particular person that I would like to speak about revealed to us in the Scriptures. That is Jeremiah the prophet in the book of Jeremiah. I can relate to this young man who warned the house of Israel. In my younger years of ministry many times when I prophesied, I would weep as I spoke the prophetic words that God gave me. I heard on numerous occasions when spiritual leaders would tell me that I was like Jeremiah. I believe what they were referring to was the brokenness that was in Jeremiah's heart over the condition of Israel. Adam Clarke gives us a little bit of insight into this prophet of God.

The Prophet Jeremiah, son of Hilkiah, was of the tribe of Benjamin. He was called to the prophetic office when very young; probably when he was fourteen years of age, and in the thirteenth of the reign of Josiah, A.M. 3375, b.c. 629. He continued to prophesy till after the destruction of Jerusalem by the Chaldeans, which took place A.M. 3416; and it is supposed that about two years after he died in Egypt.

Being very young when called to the prophetic office, he endeavored to excuse himself on account of his youth and incapacity for the work; but, being anointed by the Divine authority, he undertook the task, and performed it with matchless zeal and fidelity in the midst of a crooked and perverse people, by whom he was continually persecuted, and whom he boldly reproved, often at the hazard of his life.

His attachment to his country was strong and fervent; he foresaw by the light of prophecy the ruin that was coming upon it. He might have made terms with the enemy, and not only saved his life, but have gained ease and plenty, but he chose rather continue with his people and take his part in all the disasters that befell them.

After the destruction of Jerusalem, Nebuchadnezzar having made Gedaliah governor of Judea, the fractious Jews rose up against him, and put him to death; they then escaped to

Tahpanhes in Egypt, carrying Jeremiah with them; who, continuing to testify against their wickedness and idolatry, at length stoned the prophet to death. God marked this murderous outrage by his peculiar displeasure; for in a few years after they were all miserably destroyed by the Chaldean armies which had invaded Egypt; and even this destruction had been foretold by the prophet himself, chap. 44: "They were consumed by the sword and by the famine until there was an end of them, a small remnant only escaping," Jeremiah 44:14, Jeremiah 44:27, Jeremiah 44:28.

The pitch of desperate wickedness to which the Jews had arrived previously to their captivity was truly astonishing. They had exhausted all the means that infinite mercy, associated with infinite justice, could employ for the salvation of sinners; and they became desperately wicked; no wonder, therefore, that wrath fell upon them to the uttermost. It seems that their hardness and darkness had proceeded to such lengths that they abandoned themselves to all the abominations of idolatry to avenge themselves on God because he would not bear with their continual profligacy. Were ever people more highly favored, more desperately ungrateful, or more signally punished! What a lesson is their history to the nations of the earth, and especially to those who have been favored with the light of revelation!

The spirit of God moved in a powerful way to bring conviction upon the children of Israel through the prophet Jeremiah. Scriptures reveal the powerful influence that God's word can have upon the human heart when it is divinely inspired and spoken by holy preachers. Just this one particular subject alone could be never ending. There are many Scriptures dealing with the importance of the WORD. There are whole chapters that you and I could and should memorize and meditate upon so that the Spirit of the Lord could use us in the more powerful way.

Jeremiah 23:29 Is not my word like as a fire? Saith the Lord; and like a hammer that breaketh the rock in pieces?

Jeremiah 5:14 Wherefore thus saith the Lord God of hosts, Because ye speak this word, behold, I will make my words in thy mouth fire, and this people wood, and it shall devour them.

The Experiences of John Wesley

John Wesley (28 June 1703 – 2 March 1791) was an Anglican minister and theologian who, with his brother Charles and fellow cleric George Whitefield, is credited with the foundation of Methodism.

Very few people today are aware that John Wesley was a spirit filled man who experienced the power of the **Holy Spirit** in very real and very tangible ways. Most Methodists today are so unaware of this that if they ever experienced the Spirit in the same ways as Wesley did, they would write the experience off as emotion, science, or even as demonic before they ever considered the idea that God was interacting with them. But for Wesley, the **Holy Spirit's** power was found not only in experience but almost everything related to the Christian faith.

Whenever Wesley held outside meetings, he would tell those attending not to climb into the trees to see better. He told them that as he would be preaching many of those in attendance would fall under the power of God! It is reported that in one meeting alone over a thousand people lay out under the power of God! He reported that as he preached "people dropped on every side as if they were thunderstruck falling to the ground. Others would have convulsions exceeding all description and with many of them reported seeing visions. Some would shake like a leaf in the wind, others roared and screamed or fell with involuntary laughter."

Wesley's Journal from Jan. 1, 1739: "About sixty of our

brethren until three in the morning, the power of God came mightily upon us, insomuch that many cried out for exceeding joy, and many fell to the ground." John Wesley prayed, "Lord send us revival without its defects but if this is not possible, send revival, defects and all."

Howard A. Snyder explains that "Wesley's understanding of the church and Christian experience can be described as charismatic because of the place of the **Holy Spirit** in his theology and because of his openness to the gifts of the Spirit" (The Divided Flame 57). One will find this statement to be true just by reading Wesley's journals. He references the **Holy Spirit** time and time again. Wesley walks so closely with the Spirit that it seems he cannot be separated from God's charismatic ways of presenting Himself.

Sadly, many Christians today are offended by the same kind of charismatic works the **Holy Spirit** did in Wesley's time. This offense is not in any way new. There were very many people during Wesley's time that were also offended by the **Holy Spirit**.

That is not to say that the **Holy Spirit's** power in and of itself was offensive, but rather that those who did not believe or understand it were offended by it. That is part of the reason Wesley had a hard time with his opponents. They were people of reason who thought the **"power of the Spirit"** at these Methodist meetings was actually the power of emotion and in some instances, insanity. Wesley writes about one such situation in his journal:

We understood that many were offended at the **cries** of those on whom the power of God came, among whom was a physician, who was much afraid there might be fraud or imposture in the case. Today one whom he had known many years was the first (while I was preaching in Newgate) who broke out into **'strong cries and tears.'** He could hardly believe his own eyes and ears. He went and stood close to her, and observed every symptom, till great drops of sweat ran down her face, and all her **bones shook**. He then knew not what to think, being clearly convinced it was not fraud, nor yet any natural disorder. But when both her soul and body were healed in a moment, he acknowledged the finger of God (52-3).

This story is enough to baffle many Christians today, but even Wesley himself had experienced similar emotion and physical expression. One particular morning, he found himself in solitude when he had an encounter with the Holy Spirit. Wesley tried to put this experience into words by writing it down in his journal:

The love of God was shed abroad in my heart, and a flame kindled there, with pains so violent, yet so very ravishing, that my body was almost torn asunder. I loved. The Spirit cried strongly in my heart. I sweated. I trembled. I fainted, I sung, I joined my voice with those that excel in strength (26).

This is hardly the weirdest thing that Wesley had seen the Spirit do in His lifetime. Even though he recognized these simple physical expressions **(shaking, crying, sweating, fainting, trembling, and singing)** to be caused by the **Holy Spirit**, he had seen in Scripture and his life that the Spirit was capable of doing much, much more.

One of the popular acts of the **Holy Spirit** seen in charismatic meetings today is known as being **"slain in the Spirit."** Those who are familiar with this work recognize it when individuals fall to the ground. Once there, they typically enter either a calm state of bliss, or their body is sent into convulsions. Many understand this to be the work of the Spirit, while many others claim it to be the work of insanity. But if we look to Wesley to find an answer, we would see that he believed this to be the

power of God.

In fact, in one particular situation, a Quaker was attending one of Wesley's meetings and was growing angry with the supposed work of the Spirit going on around him. Wesley describes him as "biting his lips and knitting his brows when he dropped down as thunderstruck." God personally settled the debate for this Quaker by slaying Him. When he finally arose from the ground, he stated, **"Now I know, thou art a prophet of the Lord"** (53). This is an obvious change in mindset for this Quaker, who only moments ago was angry at what he thought to be fraud. God, however, showed him otherwise.

This is not the only time something like this has happened in Wesley's life. In a similar situation, Wesley watched some people convulse more violently than he had ever seen. Wesley prayed that God would not "suffer those who were weak to be offended," but despite his prayers, one woman was very angry. But then, Wesley documents her having "dropped down, in as violent an agony as the rest," despite her disposition towards the act. Altogether, at least 26 people endured these violent convulsions during one service on June 15, 1739.

And this is not the only time Wesley references this act of the Spirit. On April 21, of the same year, Wesley documented a man trembling violently and then sinking to the ground (50). In another situation a "three persons almost at once sunk as dead" (57). And then, on a wider scale, the Spirit performed this same type of work on New Year's Day, 1739. It was approximately three in the morning and John and Charles Wesley were in prayer with about sixty other men. Wesley wrote that *"the power of God came mightily upon us, insomuch that many cried out for exceeding joy, and many fell to the ground" (29).*

On April 26, Wesley felt the **Spirit** urge him to say **(preach)** something he had not planned on saying during one of his sermons. Wesley, certain that this was the Spirit, obeyed and as a result saw the power of God come on different individuals.

Transformed by Eating Royal Jelly

I was sensibly led, without any previous design, to declare strongly and explicitly that God 'willeth all men to be thus saved' and to pray that if this were not the truth of God, he would not suffer the blind to go out of the way; but if it were, he would bear witness to his Word. ***Immediately one and another and another sunk to the earth: they dropped on every side as Thunderstruck*** (51).

Stories similar to these are documented all over Wesley's journal, as are other works of the **Spirit**. But as these stories continued, so did the criticism. Many people still did not feel that these supernatural events were of God, and so they rejected them completely.

But despite their rejection, John Wesley saw both spiritual and emotional healing come from people's experience with God as they fell to the ground and convulsed. Many times they would rise to their feet with a true understanding of God's forgiveness of their sins. Wesley also was privileged to see actual physical healing happen. Wesley, it seems, "was convinced that the Great Physician is committed to the ultimate healing of both body and soul and that some degree of physical recovery is available even in this life—if we allow it to begin" (Maddox 147).

In one such case of physical healing, a woman by the name of Ann Calcutta "had been speechless for some time." Wesley and some others began to pray for this woman and just about as soon as they had started, her speech returned to her. She was apparently healed of some other problems too, since Wesley speaks of a fever leaving her and that "in a few days she arose and walked, glorifying God" (258).

In another story, a middle-aged woman was "restored to a sound mind." Many were able to testify that only a few days earlier she was "really distracted, and as such tied down in her bed" (100). But Wesley believed the power of the Spirit to be greater than the pain and sickness of the world, and so he prayed for this woman regardless of what many saw as a dead end. God heard the prayers of Wesley and others, and He restored the woman to health.

Even Wesley himself had experienced physical healing! On May 10, 1741, Wesley had become quite sick. He had pain in his head as well as his back, fever, and a cough that was so great that he could hardly speak. But then a miracle happened to Wesley as he "called on Jesus aloud." As he spoke, his pain disappeared, his fever left, and his strength returned. And on top of that, he felt no weakness or pain for many weeks after (194).

But perhaps one of the craziest healing miracles Wesley ever saw was at the deathbed of Mr. Meyrick, on December 20, 1742. A doctor had told Wesley that this man was not expected to make it through the night. This word was confirmed when Wesley arrived at Mr. Meyrick's side:

I went to him, but his pulse was gone. He had been speechless and senseless for some time. A few of us immediately joined in prayer. (I relate the naked fact.) Before we had done, his sense and his speech returned (306).

Wesley was obviously impressed by the finger of God upon this situation as he then wrote in his journal, "Now he that will account for this by natural causes has my free leave. But I choose to say; This is the power of God" (306). It was a miracle! God had answered prayers and raised the dead! But this was not the end of the story. Five days later, on Christmas, Mr. Meyrick was expected once again not to make it to the morning. And so, on December 25, Wesley recorded in his journal the continuation of a miracle.

I went up and found them all crying about him, his legs being cold and (as it seemed) dead already. We all kneeled down and called upon God with strong cries and tears. He opened his eyes and called for me. And from that hour he continued to recover his strength, till he was restored to perfect health. (306)

Transformed by Eating Royal Jelly

Another work of the **Spirit** that many Christians today either caution against or do not believe in is that of dreams and visions. But, just as Wesley believed in the Spirit's power to heal, slay, or simply bring a person to tears, so did he believe in the supernatural power of dreams and visions. We can read his opinion on this matter in his journal. There he includes a summary of the letters he wrote to an opponent who had advised him against believing in dreams and visions.

What I have to say touching visions or dreams is this: I know several persons in whom this great change [being free of sin to do the will of God] was wrought, in a dream, or during a strong representation to the eye of their mind, of Christ either on the cross or in glory. This is the fact; let any judge of it as they please (59).

Towards the end of his response to his opponent, Wesley grows stronger in his opinion of the existence of this work of the Spirit:""…God does now, as aforetime, give remission of sins and the gift of the Holy Ghost, even to us and to our children; yea, and that always suddenly, as far as I have known, and often in dreams or the visions of God. If it is not so, I am found a false witness before God. For these things I do, and by his grace will testify (60).

As we have seen already, the Holy Spirit made Himself known to John Wesley in many ways. But what we have not yet talked about is Wesley's involvement with the Spirit in liberating demoniacs. Christians have read in their Bible's about the Spirit's power to do such a thing, yet many today have not seen anything like it (outside of Hollywood's representation). But Wesley saw it in his own life many times.

One man, by the name of John Haydon, was reported to have been reading a sermon, when "he changed color, fell off his chair, and began screaming terribly and beating himself against the ground." Wesley arrived at the scene only to be accused by the demon as "a deceiver of the people." The demon pretended to be a manifestation of the Holy Spirit in hopes to turn people against Wesley, but Wesley fought back. He and all the others there began to pray. Soon, Haydon's "pangs ceased and both his body and soul were set at liberty" (55).

Sometimes these demonic deliverances did not take too long. For example, it only took about fifteen minutes to deliver one particular woman from "the pangs of death" (94). But other deliverances lasted much longer, such as Wesley's encounter with the young woman from Kingswood. He describes in his journal not only the physical manifestation of these demons, but he also records what the demons spoke to him (109).

I found her on the bed, two or three persons holding her. It was a terrible sight. Anguish, horror, and despair, above all description, appeared in her pale face. A thousand distortions of her whole body showed how the dogs of hell were gnawing her heart. The shrieks intermixed were scares to be endured. But her stony eyes could not weep. She screamed out, as soon as words could find their way, 'I am damned, damned; lost forever. Six days ago you might have helped me. But it is past. I am the devil's now. I have given myself to him. His I am. Him I must serve. With him, I must go to hell. I will be his. I will serve him. I will go with him to hell. I cannot be saved. I will not be saved. I must, I will, I will be damned.' She then began praying to the devil (109).

Wesley and the others with him began to sing a hymn that was popular at that time, which was written by John's brother, Charles. "Arm of the Lord, awake, awake!" they sang, which caused the demoniac to sink down immediately. But then, the demon manifested again, this time even more intensely. Charles joined John in prayer around 9:00 and together they prayed past 11:00. Over two hours were spent on this exorcism alone.
John Wesley and the Power of the Spirit
MAY 12, 2010
JAMIN BRADLEY
https://newfangled.wordpress.com/2010/05/12/john-wesley-and-the-power-of-the-Spirit/

How to Live in the Miraculous!

This is a quick explanation of how to live and move in the realm of the miraculous. Seeing divine interventions of God is not something that just spontaneously happens because you have been born-again. There are certain biblical principles and truths that must be evident in your life. This is a very basic list of some of these truths and laws:

1. You must give Jesus Christ your whole heart. You cannot be lackadaisical in this endeavour. Being lukewarm in your walk with God is repulsive to the Lord. He wants 100% commitment. Jesus gave His all, now it is our turn to give our all. He loved us 100%. Now we must love Him 100%.

My son, give me thine heart, and let thine eyes observe my ways (Proverbs 23:26).

So then because thou art lukewarm, and neither cold nor hot, I will spew thee out of my mouth (Revelation 3:16).

2. There must be a complete agreement with God's **WORD**. We must be in harmony with the Lord in our attitude, actions, thoughts, and deeds. Whatever the **WORD** of God declares in the New Testament is what we wholeheartedly agree with.

Can two walk together, except they be agreed? (Amos 3:3).

For the eyes of the LORD run to and fro throughout the whole earth, to shew himself strong in the behalf of them whose heart is perfect toward him (2 Chronicles 16:9).

3. Obey and do the **WORD** from the heart, from the simplest to the most complicated request or command. No matter what the **WORD** says to do, do it! Here are some simple examples: Lift your hands in praise, in everything give thanks, forgive instantly, gather together with the saints, and give offerings to the Lord, and so on.

> *I can of mine own self do nothing: as I hear, I judge: and my judgment is just; because I seek not mine own will, but the will of the Father which hath sent me (John 5:30).*

4. Make Jesus the highest priority of your life. Everything you do, do not do it as unto men, but do it as unto God.

> *If ye then be risen with Christ, seek those things which are above, where Christ sitteth on the right hand of God. Set your affection on things above, not on things on the earth (Colossians 3:1-2).*

5. Die to self! The old man says, "My will be done!" The new man says, "God's will be done!"

> *I am crucified with Christ: nevertheless I live; yet not I, but Christ liveth in me: and the life which I now live in the flesh I live by the faith of the Son of God, who loved me, and gave himself for me (Galatians 2:20).*

> *Now if we be dead with Christ, we believe that we shall also live with him (Romans 6:8).*

6. Repent the minute you get out of God's will—no matter how minor, or small the sin may seem.

> *(Revelation 3:19).*

> *As many as I love, I rebuke and chasten: be zealous therefore, and repent.*

7. Take one step at a time. God will test you (not to do evil) to see

if you will obey him. *Whatever He tells you to do: by His WORD, by His Spirit, or within your conscience, do it.* He will never tell you to do something contrary to His nature or His **WORD**!

> *For whosoever shall do the will of my Father which is in heaven, the same is my brother, and sister, and mother (Matthew 12:50).*

> *Then went he down, and dipped himself seven times in Jordan, according to the saying of the man of God: and his flesh came again like unto the flesh of a little child, and he was clean (2 Kings 5:14).*

ABOUT THE AUTHOR

Michael met and married his wonderful wife (Kathleen) in 1978. As a direct result of the Author and his wife's personal, amazing experiences with God, they have had the privilege to serve as pastors/apostles, missionaries, evangelist, broadcasters, and authors for over four decades. Doc Yeager has written over 80 books, ministered over 10,000 Sermons, and helped to start over 25 churches. His books are filled with hundreds of their amazing testimonies of Gods protection, provision, healing's, miracles, and answered prayers.

Websites Connected to Doc Yeager

www.docyeager.com

www.jilmi.org

www.wbntv.org

<u>Some of the Books Written by Doc Yeager:</u>

"Living in the Realm of the Miraculous #1"
"I need God Cause I'm Stupid"
"The Miracles of Smith Wigglesworth"
"How Faith Comes 28 WAYS"
"Horrors of Hell, Splendors of Heaven"
"The Coming Great Awakening"
"Sinners in The Hands of an Angry GOD",
(modernized)
"Brain Parasite Epidemic"
"My JOURNEY to HELL" - illustrated for
teenagers
"Divine Revelation of Jesus Christ"
"My Daily Meditations"
"Holy Bible of JESUS CHRIST"
"War In The Heavenlies - (Chronicles of
Micah)"
"Living in the Realm of the Miraculous #2"
"My Legal Rights to Witness"
"Why We (MUST) Gather! - 30 Biblical
Reasons"
"My Incredible, Supernatural, Divine
Experiences"
"Living in the Realm of the Miraculous #3"
"How GOD Leads & Guides! - 20 Ways"
"Weapons of Our Warfare"
"How You Can Be Healed"
"God Still Heals"
"God Still Provides"
"God Still Protects"

Made in the USA
Columbia, SC
16 September 2020